GHANA:
AN AFRICAN PORTRAIT

GHANA:
AN AFRICAN PORTRAIT.

PHOTOGRAPHS BY
PAUL STRAND

COMMENTARY BY
BASIL DAVIDSON

AN APERTURE BOOK

When Beethoven wrote his 9th Symphony, he
made it climax in a hymn to the fellowship
of Man:

"Said umschlungan, Millionen!"
May this book of ours repeat the sense and
meaning of that triumphant paean to the unity
and happiness of people everywhere.

We should like to acknowledge the help of
President Nkrumah, who did everything he could
to facilitate the making of this book, and allowed
us to feel completely at home in his country.

We also remember with graditude Bannerman
Smith, our chauffeur, who came with us on all our
travels, and served as interpreter and go-between
with great tact and intelligence, if we may judge
by the kindness of our reception everywhere.

Paul Strand

Aperture, Inc., publishes a
Quarterly of Photography, portfolios and books
to communicate with serious photographers
and creative people everywhere.
A complete catalogue will be mailed upon request.
Address: Elm Street, Millerton, New York 12546.

Book design by David Epstein.
Cover design by Stephen Korbet.
Printed by Rapoport Printing Corporation and bound
by Sendor Bindery, New York.

Manufactured in the United States of America.

PREFACE ONE AFRICA OR MANY AFRICAS?

Some time ago, Paul Strand began to think about making a portrait of Africa and its people. Other peoples had already known his penetrating candor and received his stern, affectionate gaze—among them the Mexicans and New Englanders, and in Europe the Italians, the French and the islanders of Scotland's Celtic fringe. He had also worked in Egypt and Morocco.

Now he wanted to go beyond the Sahara and find, if possible, a group of subjects that would enable him to explore and celebrate the peoples who live there in great diversity but also within an underlying unity of culture. This would be a portrait of a specific group, yet a portrait whose specificity might characterize the sub-Saharan world as a whole.

But could it be done? In setting himself this problem, Strand was being true to his lifelong humanism. He has remained among those who believe that what unites people is always more than what divides them, even if many fail to understand this, and that a future Africa, for example, will think it as reasonable and useful to recognize its own organic unity as that of any other major but united portion of the globe. One may consider this a naïve belief (it happens to be my own as well) or at least an optimistic one. Yet the imagined parallel expresses something of the mood in which we embarked on the long and various labors of making this book. And this mood, or so it now appears to me, can increasingly be seen to have its justification in reality.

True enough, it is a mood that goes against many opinions. Gone is the old colonial viewpoint, which saw only similarities and held that all Africans were very nearly the same—give or take a few local oddities or diversities. Equally gone is a variant of this vision: the pleasantly utopian belief, sometimes dear to black people in the Americas, that has assumed that all black brothers and sisters would simply fall into each other's arms if only they had the opportunity. The world has learned more about the Africans in the past quarter of a century than in all preceding time. What it has learned, perhaps above all, is that this is a family of peoples encompassing an extreme intricacy and contrast.

The land and people of Ghana, where we eventually decided to make this portrait of Africa, offers a most clear case of such complexity. Historians have written extensively of Ghana, as evidenced by an introductory reading list at the end of this volume, but still they believe they are only at the outset of their work. In 1975, for example, Ivor Wilks published a magisterial account of the country during the nineteenth century—or rather of the great kingdom of Asante (Ashanti), which during that century enclosed most of the territory of modern Ghana. His book runs to 800 dense and detailed pages. And yet Wilks found it well to remind his readers that this long labor of love and erudition is "still not intended as a comprehensive history of the Asante nation in the nineteenth century"; moreover, "in view of the quite extraordinary range and complexity of the source materials available to the student of the Asante past, it may well be many years before any definitive account of the period can—or should—be attempted."

It might be reasonable to say as much about any other large subject in African history, or even about a great many small subjects. This may be a principal reason why the study of African history has drawn the wide community of scholars now engaged upon it: the sheer diversity of African historical experience offers an endless perspective of new discoveries. A quarter of a century ago, the assertion of African history could still be useful in a world that largely ignored or denied it—to identify the forest, as it were, and even merely to insist that the forest was really there. The challenge today is to identify the trees. The trees prove unendingly numerous, and of an infinite variety of species.

All that is to the good. Yet the trees still form a forest, even if the burgeoning foliage of local studies may sometimes obscure the fact that it really is one. One can even forecast with a fair confidence of being

5

right that the historians of the next generation or so, when at last they come to the task of synthesizing the historical discoveries of the twentieth century, will be likely to emphasize Africa's underlying similarities rather than its manifold diversities. The reasons, I suggest, will emerge from two fields of African experience, the one remote and the other much more recent.

The first source of Africa's underlying unity is to be found in the facts of ancient formation. Leaving aside the infinite millennia of the Stone Age, for these defy all attempt at summary, the modern history of the Africans south of the Sahara Desert—there would have to be some obvious reservations for those north of the Desert—can be said to have begun rather more than two thousand years ago. At least as far as present knowledge goes, and present knowledge in this respect goes quite far, this was when the African societies we know today set forth upon their earliest development. Thus there began, around 300 B.C., south of the Sahara, what historians have loosely but usefully called the African Iron Age.

African populations grew in size, very slowly but also, it seems, quite steadily. Cultivation of crops, helped at least in part by iron tools that were better than stone or wooden tools, increased the food supply. More food led to larger, more stable settlement, which in turn brought the beginnings of political organization in forms that are recognizable to us, resting as they did on the division of labor and the distribution of social power.

Such settlement required for its own stability a continued process of migration. Local possibilities of producing food eventually required reduction in community population. Families or groups of families had to move away and find somewhere else to live. They migrated in those remote days into uninhabited territory, or territory occupied only by very small numbers of other people.

This process of political development expanded during and beyond the first millennium of our era, giving rise in due course to the historical communities we know today. All displayed what the anthropologist Meyer Fortes has recently called "some common institutional patterns." Here is where we find an initial source of African unity.

These common institutional patterns arose from solving common problems in comparable ways. The simplest manner of defining the similarity of patterns is to say that their political and juridical institutions were based on the idea of kinship within groups. The groups might be large or small, but they were all structured according to a system of parental loyalties. This was the type of organization which enabled the ancient Africans to multiply and master their ecology to a point where they could spread across their continent as well as survive. It acquired many specific forms, and an infinity of variants. Common to them all, however, was the notion that immanent power— we might also call it moral legitimacy—could spring from only one source. This source lay in the ancestors through whose unbroken line of succession, back to "the beginning," each people traced its link with the spiritual forces which had "made the world and all that therein is."

The point here is not that this type of organizational development did not occur in other continents, but that in Africa it formed part of a universal experience underlying what was otherwise a continued process of cultural fragmentation. This fragmentation was from unities that are only now beginning to be apprehended. One example, according to a very recent reading of archaeological evidence still far from free of perplexing gaps, is what John Sutton has called the "once prestigious, self-assured Panafrican civilisation" of fishermen and waterfolk that existed right across Middle Africa some eight thousand years ago.

Other such ancestral unities could be brought in evidence. They explain why so many of the "myths of origin" suggest so often, in their details, a common source or sources in some remote period that we can at present define only within broad dating limits. They explain why it is reasonable to speak of the arts of Africa, for example, as deriving from shared idioms of conception and expression. In short, they explain why one is justified in thinking of Africa's formative civilization in terms of a unity, despite its aspects of fragmentation. This is one reason why the faithful portrait of a single African country will also be the portrait of a much wider African scene.

A second reason, less easy to define but still insistently there, lies in the common experience of Africans in relation to the rest of the world—and above all to Europe, or at least Western Europe.

Taking a long view backwards, one can say that most of the coastal and near-coastal peoples of Africa—and, gradually, others further into the interior —began to be enclosed within the trading system of Western Europe as early as the sixteenth century. For a long time this enclosure was conducted within a relationship which left the Africans sovereign on land, just as the Europeans were sovereign on the seas.

Yet the fact remains that it was the Europeans who made the running, and who always, in the end, dominated the trade. The only important reason for this was European technological superiority, but it proved decisive.

Europe's technological superiority was small at the outset. It consisted chiefly in a capacity for ocean sailing, and in a monopoly of the manufacture of firearms. But what this meant in practice, and increasingly as time went by, was that the Europeans could offer trans-ocean markets which were otherwise closed, European goods which were otherwise unavailable and, with firearms, a new source of political power which could not be otherwise sustained. A relatively "advanced" technology confronted a relatively "backward" one—it would be out of place here to enlarge upon the history of the contrast—with the result that the first exercised a great and also growing influence. Gradually, the first came to exercise an all-pervading influence. Nothing shows this more clearly, or indeed more painfully, than Africa's active participation in the slave trade of the Europeans.

The crucial point is that for one reason or another there was little or no transfer of technology. The two trading systems remained separate, and the technological gap continued to widen. More and more Africans worked to produce more and more exports, whether human or otherwise, for the oversea system, but continued to produce them by much the same technology as before. At the same time, England went through its industrial revolution, and was followed by other countries in Europe and North America. The mercantile system gave way to the capitalist system, which, under England's lead, developed a hitherto

unprecedented productive and aggressive potential. The great Victorian century swept all before it. While kings in Africa were wondering how best they could contain these strangely imperious people on their doorsteps, the world outside their continent was changing out of recognition. By the 1850's the Europeans were beginning to arrive on the African coast in steamships; and a submarine cable linking London with Accra on the Gold Coast, that is, modern Ghana, was laid as early as 1886. There followed the invasions and subjections of the colonial period; and then the colonial period completed what the earlier mercantile enclosure had begun.

All this was a shared experience for Africans, however much the policies and practices of the various colonizing powers might differ in emphasis or impact. The chief result, no doubt, was to make whatever happened in Africa subject to whatever might happen in Western Europe. Deprived of power, the Africans were taken out of their own history. And when, around the middle of our own century, the Africans once more began to reenter their own history, they did so with a new baggage of ideas. No matter how vividly they might recall their own past, how staunchly they might adhere to their own traditions and beliefs, the path to independence could follow no other route but the one laid down by the Europeans; that is, by way of the ideas and loyalties of the European nation-state. And so it was that some forty colonies were relaunched as some forty nations. The pattern could only be a recipe for trouble, but no other pattern was to hand. Modern history, like ancient history, again combined to give the Africans a unity of experience.

So it was that we decided in the early 1960's, in the somewhat smaller matter of this book, that a portrait of Ghana could also be a portrait of Africa. Talking it over at Orgeval, we saw that there were some special grounds for choosing Ghana. Time and convenience of access and movement were factors not to be ignored. Ghana is a fairly average-sized African country, about two hundred miles wide and six hundred long; even in the 1960's its communications system was by no means bad. Still more usefully, Ghana contains a diversity of climate, vegetation, and a corresponding cultural and economic pattern that is broadly representative of the three major zones into which most of West Africa is horizontally divided: a narrow coastal plainland, a zone of tall rain forest, and a northerly country ranging from sparse woodland to treeless savanna. From another angle, the people of Ghana have been vigorous makers of history during the past three or four hundred years. If Ghana's older history is linked inseparably with that of the whole western part of the African continent, its newer history has marked the great initial chapters of Africa's participation in the modern world.

There were some contingent reasons. It happened that the late President Kwame Nkrumah had known me since 1952, when I had first visited his country, and welcomed the idea that Paul and Hazel Strand should work in Ghana. In due course the Strands embarked on their journey and found a sympathetic and intelligent welcome. They explained their plans, and these plans were approved. At first they settled for a while in Accra so as to gain a sense of the country. Then they began to travel. And they traveled enormously, for some ten thousand miles over a matter of four months, with Strand photographing as they went or deciding upon subjects that he would return to later.

Perhaps I may add that the making of this book, even then, had only begun. The Strands went home to Orgeval, where they passed another six months or so in developing plates and working on prints. Some time later it appeared that Strand would make his final selection from about four hundred prints. But how to choose them? We took to laying out prints on the floor, a dozen at a time, to see what they "did to each other." This was Paul's invariable phrase: "Prints do something to each other, and you have to see what." A long process: it continued, off and on, for months. After that, Michael Hoffman brought his seeing eye, and more and better changes were made.

Thus there is nothing in the least haphazard about the selection and the sequence of these photographs. They are first and foremost a portrait of Ghana, above all of the Ghana that Nkrumah led to independence. But in ways that may be intimate and profound they are also a portrait of the Africa within which Ghana has taken shape.

My aim here has been to deepen this portrait without, as it were, repeating it. I wrote this essay independently of the photographs, but keeping them very much in mind. Our idea was to offer the kind of information, reaching back into the past, looking at the present, having the future not entirely out of mind, that would illuminate the photographs: just as the photographs, in their turn, would illuminate the text. In other words, we thought of the book that should emerge as one that could yield a continual and meaningful counterpoint between photographs and text, each standing in its own right, but each the richer for its companion.

I began thinking about my essay while selection of the photographs was still in process, and for me, too, the difficulty was one of selection. What facts? What sources? What manner of text? I finished thinking about all this a good deal later. But where I began was a place called Wa, and I should like to begin here by telling about that. For Wa opens a useful window on the scene besides taking you to the place where this essay was conceived.

ONE THE VIEW FROM WA

The thinking of a book, as distinct from the writing, may get itself started in all manner of places, and for reasons far from obvious. The luck of a chance encounter, a certain atmosphere conducive to reflection:

all such things can play their part. So will less subjective matters such as satisfactory cooking, slow tropical afternoons, the soft dusk hours that lift away the heat and breathe with a wind from the forest, and, together with all these, time which has no clocks.

Now, all these things are blessedly present, as it happens, in a small town of northern Ghana called Wa, and Wa was the place where this book really got itself started in my mind: Wa the peaceful, Wa the reflective, Wa the place to think about a book that one eventually will want to write.

It is not the obvious place to begin a book about Ghana. Accra would perhaps be that: a big commercial town which has grown out of a small colonial settlement in little more than thirty years, and now contains within itself most of the elements that go to make this country what it is—a population where you may easily find members of all Ghana's principal peoples and hear all of its five chief languages, altogether a city where the drive and pace of change and growth are insistently present. Or else one might expect to begin thinking about Ghana in one or another of its smaller coastal towns or villages, along a seaboard where the high surf piles and runs upon sands and beaches fine enough to make the tourist fortune of any European country, and where men from Europe first came ashore five centuries ago. Or in venerable Kumase, the old capital of the Asante kingdom; or in Tamale, administrative center of the northern plains. But not, or not at all expectably, in Wa.

Yet there is one powerful reason, aside from peace and quiet and slumbering tradition, why it is good to begin looking at Ghana from Wa or from one of its neighboring towns of the far north. Viewing Ghana from here, one sees this country in its continental setting: not, that is, as a land which history has approached from the sea, but as one belonging to all that community of African countries which link their way southward, one after another, from the far Sahara and the reed-fringed waters of Lake Chad, or the ports of the inland Niger and the spacious grasslands, to the forests that lie behind the coast and to the coast itself. Through most of the years of its long formation, Ghana has belonged to the varied and dynamic civilization of that great inland country, while the sea was

no more than its empty hinterland. Only the last two centuries have really altered this, and the alteration has remained at most a partial one. To understand Ghana, one needs to remember that its framework is the wide interior of Western Africa.

Wa has another advantage for the traveler. If you reach it from the coast, as probably you will, you pass almost through the length of Ghana. On this occasion I went there myself with a learned pilgrim, al-Hajji Osmanu of Kintampo, who joined me because he was in search of privately held rare manuscripts that he might acquire, or at any rate copy, for the Institute of African Studies of the University of Ghana. There could be few more fortunate companions, whether for modesty and wit or for learning and long experience. Al-Hajji Osmanu has traveled much. At a future time, he told me, he would like to go to Beirut, where he has many friends who are Muslim scholars like himself, and he would also like to visit Jerusalem so as to pay his respects to the memory of Abraham. But just now he was searching for rare books and writings in Ghana itself; besides, the time was the end of Ramadan, and he was tired from its fasting and the loss of sleep which Ramadan entails for the devout. A little change would do him good.

So I drove up from Accra with another Ghanaian at the wheel and looked for the pilgrim in his forest home of Kintampo, some two hundred miles to the north of the capital. The driver was Francis, who comes himself from the south, though there is nothing practical and sensible that Francis does not know about traveling in any part of Ghana. Moreover, as a veteran of the British Army in the Second World War, Francis played a part in early nationalist strivings, so that he is well aware of a great deal about the politics of Ghana over the past twenty years—and about the politics of other countries, too. Planted on a firm sense of humor and a shrewd understanding of mankind, Francis also has his full share of Ghanaian tolerance and laughter.

We left Accra fairly early in the morning: not as early as we had decided the night before and yet, according to custom, just as early as we had really intended. Soon after nine o'clock we were high in the hills behind Accra. From here you have the coastal plains in full view. They are fertile and full of villages and towns, a blue-brown mist of lowland where many little states and armies, and a few big ones, have clashed and flourished in the distant past, and where new industries now raise their first slim stacks and girders. Once over the top of this scarp, you have a little range of hills, another dip into the plains and then, climbing steadily, the long northward pull into the forests of Asante.

Here the skylines disappear behind the tall jungle of trees, and the road narrows to a green canyon paved with asphalt running between red earth. This is the land of cocoa, first grown here on any scale some eighty years ago, but it is also the land of yams and pineapples, cassava, coffee, and other characteristic harvests. Beneath the towering cotton woods and their lesser neighbors, the little farms seem at first a mere confusion of plants and stalks that are hard to distinguish from one another, with cassava growing in the shade of wide banana palms, and cocoa bushes nestling in the striped sunlight as though put down haphazardly and left to grow like weeds. But the apparent confusion is misleading. Like much else in Africa, things are by no means what they seem. This is in fact a highly skilled farming peculiar to the forest country. Many of these farms are models of good cultivation.

Toward Kumase the forest thins a little but the town still seems encradled by enormous trees: a town of prosperous markets fed by a multitude of hidden villages to the point where it sometimes looks like a great village itself. This, too, is a misleading impression. Kumase is in fact a city with a proud and valorous reputation, and has been such for more than two hundred years. Here you may find many interesting things and meet many interesting people. But Francis and I had far to go. We started out again soon after dawn.

Mist lay over the Asante hills that morning. Immense trees hung above the road like the shadows of ancestral ghosts. Creepers dangled legendary ladders such as those that, according to Asante myth, once linked God with the world of men. Hilltops opened briefly across seas of woodland where the farmers of Gyaaman and Brong produce cocoa that goes to half the world, and where, long ago, the little

gold mines of the Middle Ages fed the trans-Saharan trade. We went up through Mampong and Ejura, and forked left for Nkoranza and Kintampo, with the good road leaping out behind us in plumes of pale brown dust.

Arriving at Kintampo, we find al-Hajji Osmanu. We do not find him at home, in the midst of a numerous and bustling family who give us their greetings, but out upon his farm. We find him looking at his cassava. He is walking in a field, a slender figure in a long white robe beneath a large black umbrella which he holds aloft in his left hand. He waves and comes toward us with the careful lack of haste that good manners demand of friends who meet after an absence. His small brown eyes gleam an appropriately courteous welcome. The crops? Well, the crops are as they may be, neither better nor worse. The journey to the north? But of course: he is ready to depart at once.

And we do indeed depart at once, returning to his home only to gather a mat and cooking pot and other traveler's gear, after which Francis turns the car northward again. Here the road leads up to the chain ferry over the Black Volta. This is no longer the forest country: now you are out on the edge of the plains of the Sudan, a vast and echoing region that links the Atlantic to the waters of the Nile, with no more than an occasional tall mountain or a little ridge of hills to interrupt its far horizons.

The ferry goes over the Black Volta with a sudden clutter of traffic and the squawk of captive chickens on their way to market, and afterwards the road continues through the old state of Gonja, founded here by warrior chiefs in the late sixteenth century, and runs through several scattered towns and villages until it reaches the local capital, which is Wa. We turn into Wa not long after nightfall and find beds in the government rest house, a neat cluster of conical huts that are whitewashed within and without, and are roofed with thatch.

We settle into Wa, and Wa, as I have said, is a quiet place. But Wa is also a place of dignity and discrimination, the Africa of yesterday and the Africa of today. And then, again, Wa is what it sounds like, a trifle seedy, somewhat out of date, liable to be surprised: rural, not to say rustic, in its manners and appearance. Here in this country town, at any rate, you are thoroughly in Africa; for those with the patience to teach themselves to read it, Wa is as good as a guidebook to the continent.

I sit down in Wa by the waters of memory, and think about the problems of what I am going to write. Wa is good for thinking; again because it is a quiet place. But the quietness of Wa is the noise of Africa. There is really no such thing as quietness here, yet the noise of Africa is different from ours. With us you achieve quietness by shutting doors and windows against a background of noise that is likely to be loud, continuous, and disconcertingly impersonal. Nobody in Africa shuts doors and windows (although the cloistered habit is growing in the cities), and the immediate foreground is likely to be loud with a great deal of highly personal noise. People shout powerfully to each other. Children explode in swarms. Especially after nightfall the insect population, multifarious in number and variety, begins communing with itself in a relentless code of penetrating Morse transmission, so that a single cicada will sound like a ship's radio, and even the marching feet of ants may seem to whisper like the armies of the night. Yet behind this piercing foreground tumult there is a background silence, and this is the quietness of Wa and the silence of Africa. The oldest and worst of trucks will erupt in painful horror, right there beneath your window; but it will go away, and when it goes away this background silence will swallow it entirely.

There is nothing to do in Wa, and yet there is everything to do. The boredom is complete and unrelieved, and yet you've scarcely a moment to call your own. After a while you forget the meaning of boredom, an alien thing belonging to clocks and careers, and settle down to the enjoyment of the present.

It is desirable, for example, to pay a call on the Wa Na, traditional potentate of the ancient polity called Gonja. He inhabits a handsome palace of whitewashed clay, and there you offer him your respects with a customary gift of one pound sterling. (I forget to bring it with me, but the pilgrim makes a surreptitious loan.) It is also interesting to pay a visit to the Chief Butcher, oldest and most venerable of the elders of Wa, an energetic young patriarch of some ninety summers whose title indicates high status in these parts. He is determined to keep up with his position, and is now again contemplating marriage, though already possessing more sons and grandsons than he can easily remember. His prospective bride brings us beer —the *pito* that is brewed from millet and is tea-brown in color, souplike in consistency, faintly alcoholic— and the Chief Butcher speaks of her with a gleaming though somewhat beady-eyed benevolence. She is not yet old enough to marry, he explains, but will be soon. A sturdy maiden, she is perfectly at ease. It is, of course, an honor to be chosen by the Chief Butcher, and the profits will be handsome. Many servitudes remain in Africa; this is one of them.

It is instructive as well as pleasant to spend many hours with the assembled scholars of Wa, who meet beneath a spreading conference tree; all this, again, is the Africa of yesterday which is also, persistently and problematically, the Africa of today. And then in the evenings, after nightfall has brought its cool breeze from the northern desert, there are ceremonies of a different kind: foregatherings in one or another of the bars of Wa, where European beer can be consumed *al fresco*—and is consumed, in quantities appropriate to this thirst-promoting place. Then you may discuss with the local magistrate, or the local schoolmaster, or the local government official, or any visitor who may happen to be there the Africa of today which is also, persistently and problematically, the Africa of yesterday.

And after that, vaguely in its natural order, there is the question of supper. It comes in various forms. Now and then it comes by the hand of George, a son of Hajji Osmanu's who is also living here in Wa. George is about twelve years old and is pretty much, already, in the Africa of tomorrow. He arrives on a new bicycle with a lump of raw beef wrapped snugly in a palm leaf. "From Hajji," he explains. Handing it over, he adds: "Okay, I will go now." And go he does, pedaling into the darkness with a confident scrunch of tires. I give this beef to the cook, a craftsman of years and wisdom, and he grills it in an outhouse where there is an ancient stove whose metal label carries the mystic words CALEDONIA NEW DOVER and also, with a gentle reassurance you may be glad to

(continued on page 121)

The past

Is but the cinders of the present;

The future

The smoke

That escaped

Into the cloud-bound sky . . .

The Search, Kwesi Brew

"Once upon a time Ananse the Great Spider
collected all the wisdom in the world and shut
it up in a gourd, and was climbing up a tree to
deposit it on the top. He got into difficulties,
however, before he reached half-way up, as he
had tied a gourd on to his belly, and it hindered
him from climbing properly. His son, Ntikuma,
who was watching him, said, 'Father, if you had
really all the wisdom of the world with you,
you would have had sense enough to tie the gourd
on your back.' His father, seeing the truth
of this, threw down the gourd in a temper.
It broke, and the wisdom it contained became
scattered, and men came and picked up what
each could carry away."

A story from Asante

"I shall sleep in white calico;

   War has come upon the sons of men

   And I shall sleep in calico;

   Let the boys go forward,

   Kple and his people should go forward;

   Let the white man's guns boom,

   We are marching forward;

   We shall sleep in calico . . ."

Song of War, Kofi Awoonor

33

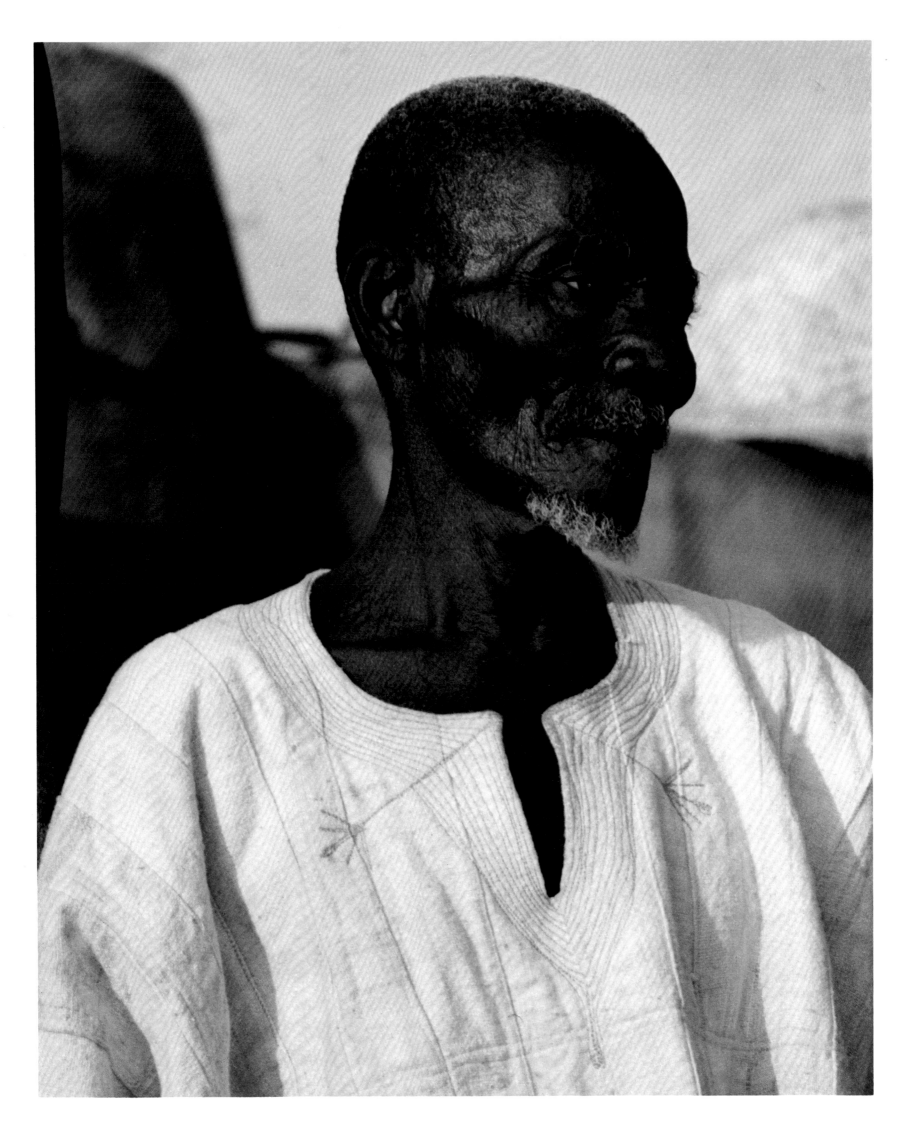

"Give me black souls
  Let them be black
  Or chocolate brown
  Or make them the
  Colour of dust
  Dustlike
  Browner than sand
  But if you can
  Please keep them black
  Black

"Give me some drums
  Let them be three
  Or may be four
  And make them black
  Dirty and black
  Of wood
  And dried sheepskin
  But if you will
  Just make them peal
  Peal . . ."

African Heaven, Frank Kobina Parkes

42

"None but kings
and great men trade here,
the same as myself."

The Asantehene Osei Bonsu in 1820

"Tell him that

We do not wish for greediness

We do not wish that he should curse us

We do not wish that his ears should be hard of hearing

We do not wish that he should call people fools

We do not wish that he should act on his own initiative

We do not wish things done as in Kumase

We do not wish that it should ever be said 'I have no time, I have no time'

We do not wish personal abuse

We do not wish personal violence . . .

Admonitions to Ghanaian chiefs on being enstooled

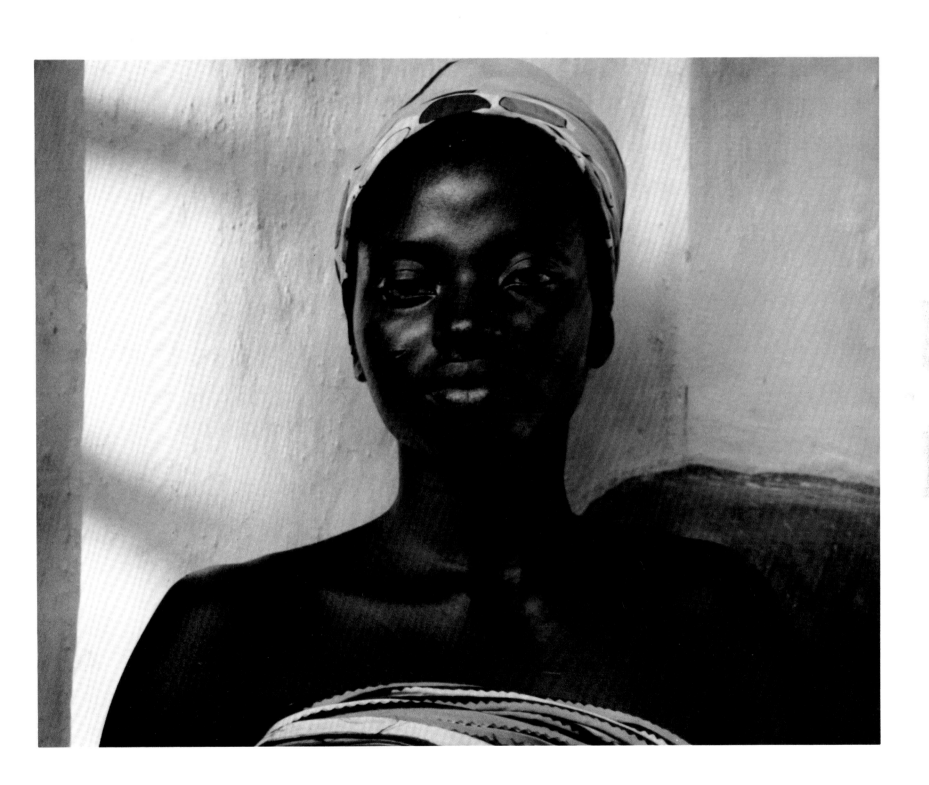

When you have no master,
someone will catch you and sell
you for what you are worth.

Asante maxim

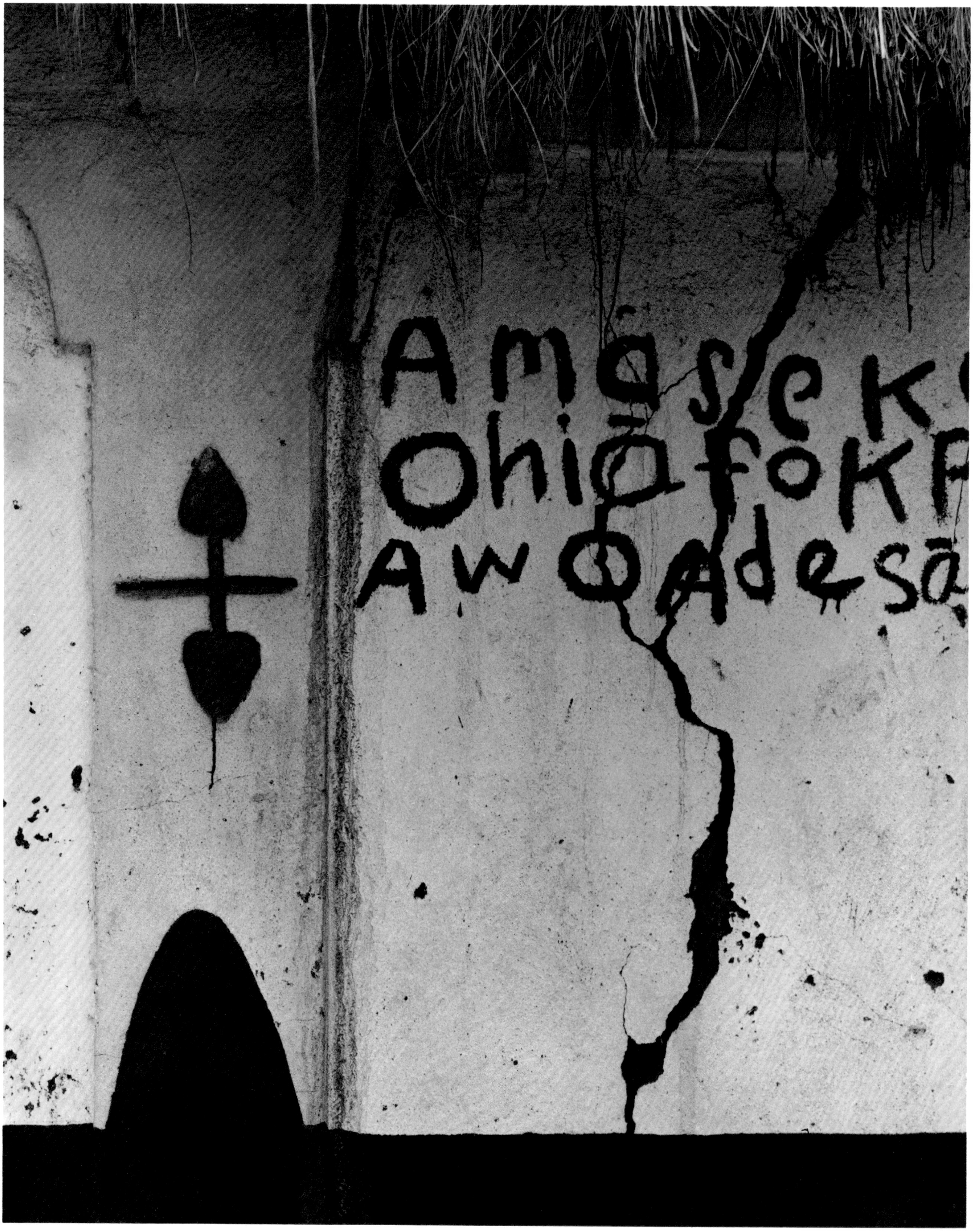
Amasek
Ohiãfok
Awoadesã

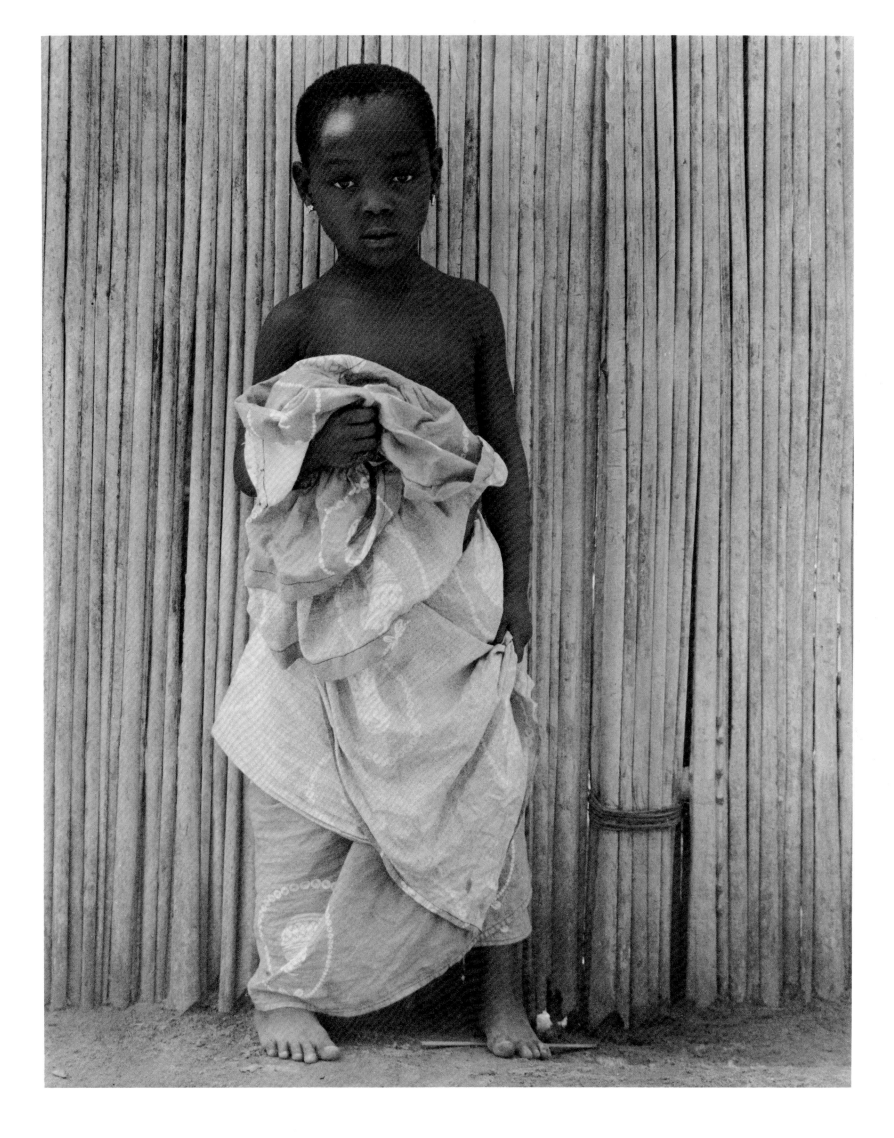

"The European merchant is my shepherd.
   And I am in want;
   He maketh me to lie down in cocoa farms;
   He leadeth me beside the waters of great need;
   He restoreth my doubt in the pool parts . . .

"The general managers and profiteers frighten me.
   Thou preparedst a reduction in my salary
   In the presence of my creditors.
   Thou anointedst my income with taxes;
   My expense runs over my income.
   Surely unemployment and poverty will follow me
   All the days of my poor existence,
   And I shall dwell in a rented house for ever!"

A Gold Coast soldier's parady of Psalm 23

"I strolled along the Garfield avenue,

Past Knight, and the black abandoned pit latrine,

To where, way back, a bathroom could be seen,

But now, a barn house garage stands, all new.

Behind me, was the road to Damascus;

Before, the College blocks, and a water-tower:

And as I walked, I saw a Lazarus

Emerge from a tomb, his dead-clothes o'er his shoulder.

His powerful body freed from bandages,

A rising flame of life, from the night of death.

Uncertain yet how long the ravages,

The germs, and the million killing ways of earth

Will spare his new-found Life, his radiant grace.

And as he walked past me, I saw my face.

A Second Birthday, Albert Kayper Mensah

"So shall we say
  Shall we put it this way
  Shall we say that the maid of Kyerefaso,
  Foruwa, daughter of the Queen-mother was
  as a young deer, graceful in limb. Such she
  was, with head held high, eyes soft and
  wide with wonder. And she was light of foot,
  light in all her moving . . .

"So shall we say
  Shall we put it this way, that
  all the village butterflies, the men, tried to
  draw near her at every turn, crossed and
  crossed her path, and said of her,
  'She shall be my wife, and mine, and
  mine, and mine' . . ."

New Life at Kyerefaso, Efua Theodora Sutherland

80

When the assembly broke up,
Konaduwa hastened away, meaning
to go to Asiakwa to report
the case to the District Commissioners.
But at Anyiman the Birem had
overflowed its banks, and the ferryman
exacted a toll of sixpence from
every passenger. When Konaduwa
was asked by one of the ferrymen to pay
the amount, she parted her lips in
a brilliant smile, displaying her teeth,
which had a gap at the centre of
the upper row.

"What exceptionally fine teeth
this woman has!" the ferryman exclaimed.
"Keep your sixpence," he added,
"and I will pay it for you."

Konaduwa thanked him with
a bow, and tied the coin up in a corner
of her handkerchief . . .

Konaduwa's Trial, E. E. Obeng

"At the start of the affair, they came

Peacefully,

With soft sweet talk.

'We've come to trade,' they said,

'To reform the beliefs of the people,'

'To halt oppression here below, and theft,'

'To clean up and overthrow corruption.'

Not all of us grasped their motives,

So now we've become their inferiors.

They deluded us with little gifts

And fed us tasty foods . . .

But recently they've changed their tune . . ."

Nazm al-la'ali bi-akhbar wa tanbih al-kiram,
'Umar of Kete-Krache (northern Ghana), 1900–01

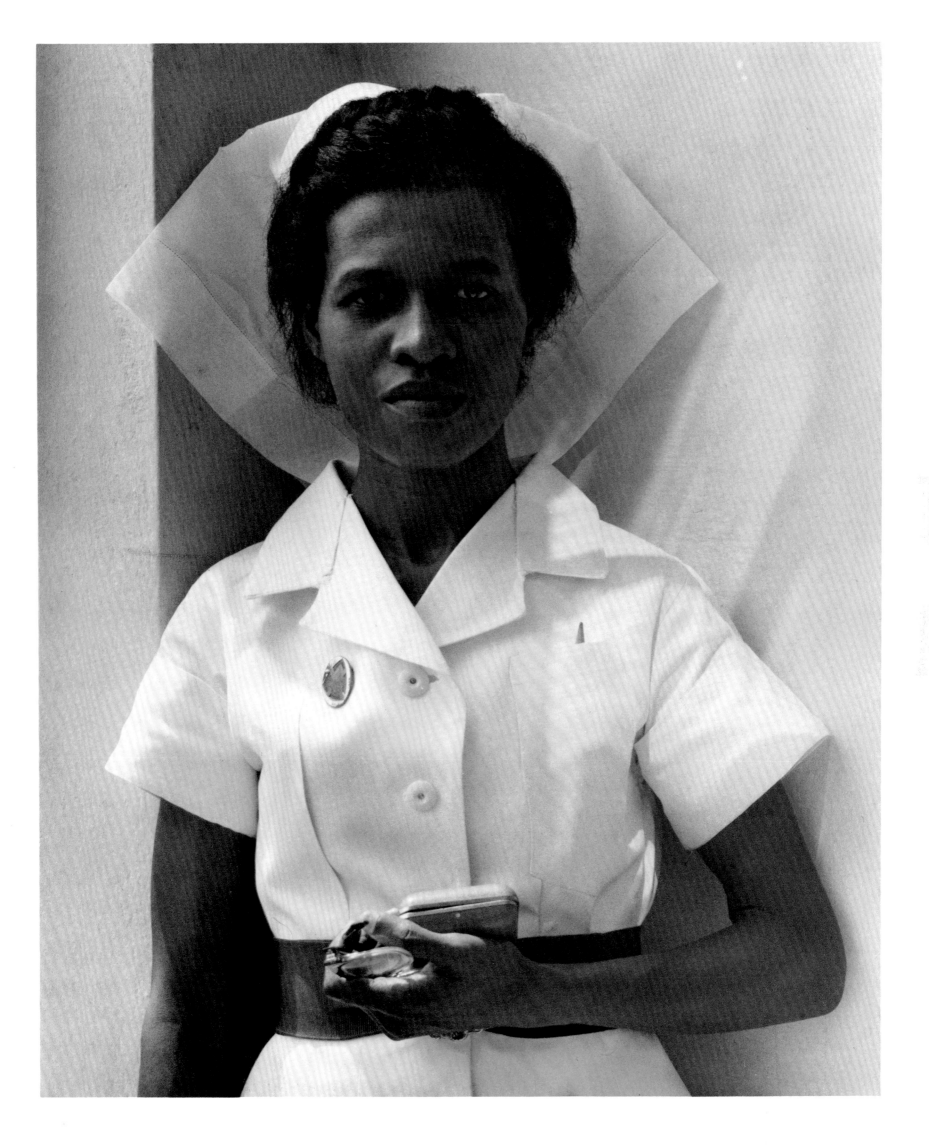

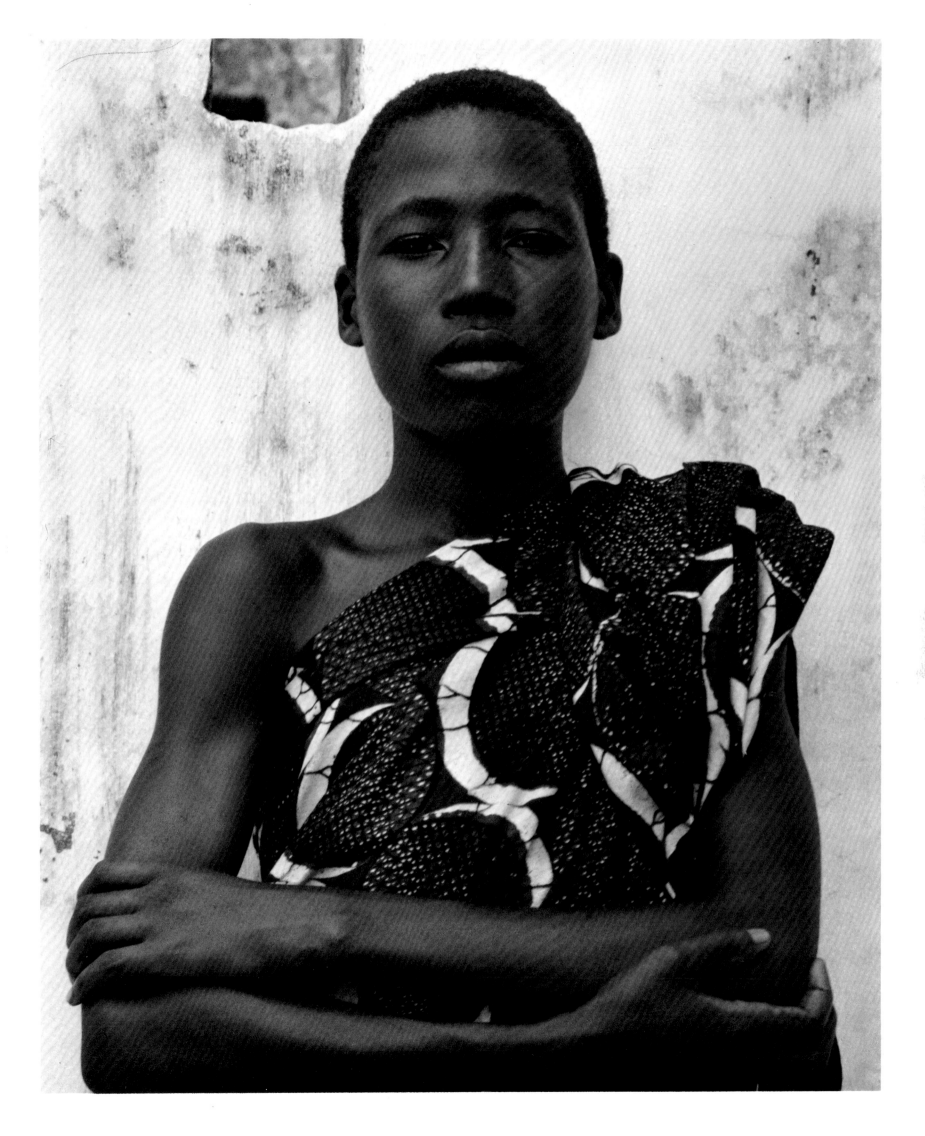

"With union, our example
of a multiple of peoples living
and working for mutual
development in amity and
peace will point the way for the
smashing of inter-territorial
barriers existing elsewhere, and
give a new meaning to the concept
of human brotherhood."

Kwame Nkrumah, *Africa Must Unite*

There is nothing
as important as wealth

Ghanaian maxim

"River, I am passing

   Ogyamma fruits are ripe, calling upon
      farmers to mark out their farms,

New settlers have gone to start
      new farmsteads

The palm fronded shed on the bank calls me

The monkey has espied from the tree tops
      what is approaching

The eagle has seen afar through the telescope,

Civilisation and inventions ushering in
      calamity, but

River, I am passing . . ."

          Afram, Andrew Amankwa Opoku

Photographs

have, THE NEW EPICURE. They are hopeful names, but the cook has mastered this stove with all the cunning of an artist who has long endured the cooking of the Europeans; and the results are satisfactory.

There is peace and sleep, and then there is breakfast. This is sometime after dawn, the morning of another day; and with it comes Ansenah Wara, bringing gifts of nuts and apples and bananas, and the talk of this other day that is the same day and yet an altogether different one. Ansenah Wara is a lady of powerful character and unaging beauty, as you may see from Strand's portrait of her (page 105), but she is also a great deal more than that. She is one of the local founders of modern politics, the politics of national-ism and of independence. She has within her memory the facts that really matter: the difficult beginning, when the ideas of this new age were words that meant nothing or could not be true; the slow and painful labor of explaining, when these words began to mean something and could possibly be true; the steady on-ward movement of acceptance when they came to represent the only central and important truth; and then, at last, the back-and-forth battle between the future and the past. Ansenah Wara reviews all this over breakfast, funding nuts and apples from a basket that is never empty, and says that she is only sorry, nearing seventy, that she has not yet found the time to learn to read and write.

In this way and in that, the hours in Wa speed past in a whirl of talk and quickened memories; and somehow or other, in this way and in that, the prob-lem is solved; and my text, for better or for worse, begins to be there.

The chapters that now follow are a brief but, I hope, balanced account of the history of Ghana, and of the background to its present scene and develop-ment. They are not a commentary on the photo-graphs, much less a travelog. They do not tell you how the photographs were taken, or even where they were taken. All the same, they belong to the photo-graphs: just as the photographs belong to them.

TWO A VERY OLD NEW COUNTRY: UNITY IN DIVERSITY

Looking south from Wa, one can divide Ghana into several regions. There are the grasslands of the north, then the country of the tropical forest, further south the plains and small hills that lie near the coast, and finally the coast itself. Yet this rough division barely serves even to suggest this country's diversity of cul-ture, language and historical tradition. Let us, as a pre-liminary, outline some of that diversity.

As to languages, the Ghana Broadcasting Serv-ice has used as many as eight, including English, for its transmissions. Of these, the most important local lan-guage is one or another version of Twi, pronounced approximately *Tch-vee* (the "w" in Twi, as in Ewe, deriving from the orthography of German or Swiss-German missionaries who first wrote these words). Like Hausa or Swahili, Lingala or seSotho in other African lands, Twi is something of a *lingua franca* in that most Ghanaians either know it well or under-stand enough for daily intercourse. Perhaps Twi will one day follow English as the official language of the population, which numbers now about nine million.

Many of Paul Strand's photographs illustrate Ghanaian variations in appearance and manner of life. These variations are reflected in a multitude of ways. Some of them are religious. In old Africa, politics and religion went closely hand in hand, so that each separate people evolved its own separate religion. Even today, the union of politics and religion remains important, although the old age of faith passes rapidly away under pressures of the modern world. Long misunderstood by outside observers as little more than foolish superstition, these religions are now seen to have possessed—and, here and there, still to possess—a strong systemic power, depth of concept, and cohesive social value. They established standards of moral behavior. They "explained" the world as well as instructed men and women how to live in it. They guarded the rights of the individual, but also those of the community. They served as "spiritual charters" whose intention was to discourage violence and greed, impose sanctions on criminals, and ease the flow of daily life. We have learned to look beyond their shrines and altars, so well portrayed in some of Strand's photographs, to the beliefs and ideas which stand behind them.

As for the world religions, Islam came into these lands about six centuries ago but made little progress, except in the far north, until the nineteenth century. Those who brought it were mostly traders. Working as middlemen in the trade which joined the plains with the forest, and the forest with the coastland, they established markets such as Wa. They made few converts outside their own kind, but conserved their faith. Their learned men, their 'ulama, founded schools of Quranic instruction, assembled manuscript libraries, and themselves wrote memoirs and essays on Muslim law, or compiled lists of ancestral descent and other characteristic works, including a few histories. Even today the 'ulama of Wa maintain a Quranic school which provides a two-year course in religious and moral instruction for about one hundred pupils at a time.

Here in the north, the 'ulama have remained integrally part of the Muslim culture of the Western Sudan as it was in the past, and as it is today; and it would be absurd to see them in any way as isolated survivors from a shipwrecked civilization, or as refugees from a time that is gone. Hajji Osmanu, with whom I traveled to Wa, is a good example. Joyful and enterprising, he is fully heir to the venerable tradition of wandering scholarship that has existed here for many centuries, a system by which the aspirant to

erudition goes from one acknowledged master to the next, studying with each for a sufficient time until he himself can set up as teacher, and meanwhile earning his living at a useful trade. Hajji Osmanu had stayed in Mecca and Medina during his pilgrimage for a long enough time to become a qualified plumber. Now he has given up plumbing and found a more congenial occupation as what he calls a "fisher for documents," a collector of Islamic texts for the archives of Ghana's chief university. But he does this "fishing" with the same happy sense of its all being as much a part of life as fixing drains or water pipes. He enjoys his work. He respects himself and his traditions. He doesn't think of history as something outside his own life.

Christianity first came with the Portuguese along the coast at the end of the fifteenth century, but made few converts for another three and a half centuries. When conversions at last became more numerous, along the seaboard and across the coastal plains, they went together with the European education that missionaries could offer, so that the early history of national strivings here is often inseparable from the learning gained in mission schools. Today, Christianity makes more converts than it did, though fewer than Islam.

Yet the sap and savor of Africa's cultures lie neither in the Muslim nor the Christian tradition, but in that of indigenous belief and custom. Of all this, proverbs and popular sayings can tell interesting things, and in Ghana they abound. A collection made a century ago by an African missionary of German-Swiss formation shows these proverbs as they were before the days of European rule. Often they are much the same in meaning as the popular sayings of other lands, yet even when their meaning is the same their expression stays pungently local: "When a great number of mice dig a hole, it fails to become deep"; or, more personally, "On the honeymoon the yams are always sweet"; and, more sardonically, "Though your sister's thigh may be plump, it is not you who will lie on it."

These are sayings of Asante, of the forest country of the central part of Ghana—the country, together with its neighboring coastal plains, that has really formed the heartland of Ghana, for it is here that major peoples have lived and developed their own civilization since remote antiquity. This is where most of the population lives, and it is here, above all, that the Asante and the Fante and other branches of Akan people who live in the plains and forests—as well as the Ewe, who live beyond the Volta River, and the Ga, who founded the city of Accra—have given their unmistakable imprint to Ghanaian life. This is the homeland of many things that immediately attract a visitor's attention: traditional dancing and its modern variants such as "high life"—one English usage among many which speak for the chuckle in these peoples' ideas about themselves—and the brilliance of the rhythm of drums; golden-threaded *kente* cloth; shrines and altars and the ritual pouring of libations to the memory of ancestors in liquid which must, if possible, be gin.

Much about Ghanaian life and history is also revealed by the plastic arts, but especially by metal sculpture, in which Ghanaians occupy a distinctive place in the "family" of such arts in Western Africa. Perhaps their best-known sculptural form, or at least the one most prized by collectors, has consisted in the brass weights for weighing gold dust that the Asante, in particular, have made and used for many centuries. Little can be said with any certainty about the origin of these weights. That they began to be made and used when the trans-Saharan trade was still of more general importance than the southern coastal trade is indicated by the fact that the oldest weights were matched to Muslim measures. This would mean that such weights were in use before the seventeenth century, perhaps long before. But their interest does not lie in their age. It lies in their workmanship and in the persons or objects they depict: a large collection of them can offer the discriminating eye a range of "ideas" and "scenes" that have much to tell of traditional culture here.

In the sculpture of wood, the forest and coastal peoples—the Akan in their various branches—have given particular attention to the making of fine stools, generally with a curved rectangular seat supported by a pillar which may be about twelve inches high. Stools are important in Ghana (as among some other African peoples near and far) for two reasons, one obvious and the other immanent. The obvious reason is that stools are what chiefs must sit on—one need hardly add that ordinary people also use stools—if they are to exercise their authority. The immanent and larger reason is that the stools of chiefs represent the legitimate inheritance of authority: the persons change, but the stools do not. They "contain," as it were, an accredited power; and it is out of respect for this ancestral power that chiefly stools are made with care and distinction. So it is, again, that kings or great chiefs are "enstooled," and that the kings of Asante, when creating a new department of government, used to create an appropriate stool with a corresponding title for it.

Much that belongs to the traditions of the past has gone from the scene. But much else remains powerfully alive—far more, indeed, than will become apparent at first sight—while even that which changes does so in a manner which befits a people of confidence and optimism. Foreigners who move around Ghana, and not only Ghana, will not be likely to think that the notion of an "African personality" is merely a hopeful slogan. Whatever the real content of that term may be, there is certainly a Ghanaian personality. Few who travel in Ghana fail to be impressed by it. They may find Ghanaians exhausting in their energy, pigheaded in their opinions, and unpredictable in their politics; they will also find them staunch friends, good companions, and altogether a people with a talent for making the best of life.

After 1957, these people set about building a new country for themselves. They have found their way through many difficulties and now face many more. Yet their progress in modernizing their country has not been small. Everywhere there are signs of it—in new cities, schools, universities, social services, dams, harbors, power grids, industries and manufactures. All this represents an achievement which rests in turn on the kind of people that history has fashioned here. Ghanaians are accustomed to beginning any new enterprise by pouring a libation to the ancestors "who brought us into the world, who watch over us while we are here, and who will receive us when we die." Let us follow suit by pouring a libation, even if a modest one, to the ancestors of modern Ghana.

THREE GHANA IN HISTORY

The lush and ever-crowding forest of the tropics tells much about the past of Ghana, especially if one remembers that in ancient times this forest covered more of the country than it does today. Here people have lived in small or fairly small communities, often isolated from each other save for the communication of pathways amid the trees; and they have had to face and solve some special and occasionally very tough problems of survival. They have had to work out techniques of forest cultivation. They have had to learn to live with the malarial mosquito and the tsetse fly, which kills cattle and gives men sleeping sickness, as well as with other carriers of mortal fever.

Yet the history of human habitation in these ancient forests is extremely old: just how old, we do not yet know, except that it goes back into remote Stone Age times. Some idea of its antiquity may be gained from the opinion of linguistic experts, who consider that the parent tongue of the family of spoken languages—sometimes called the Niger-Congo family—began dividing into the parents of existing languages as far back as ten thousand years ago. But it appears fairly certain that the men and women who spoke those parent languages were few in number and multiplied into significantly large populations only a long time afterwards. This period of multiplication is generally thought to have begun with an increase in food supplies which, as we have noted, corresponds more or less with the use of iron for tools and weapons.

When did the Ghanaian Iron Age, the age of regular cultivation, begin? Not far from the city of Accra towards the northeast, where the hills which channel the Volta River rise from their coastal plains, there is a steep-sided spur of land called Adwuku. Here the archaeologists of modern Ghana have located signs of long settlement by vanished populations who knew how to find, smelt and forge iron. Working from the broken pottery and other artifacts that strew this hilltop, archaeologists have distinguished two main periods before A.D. 1600, and the first is thought

to have come to an end around the twelfth century. But it seems reasonable to think that Iron Age folk were living in the coastal hills a good deal more than a thousand years ago.

Other evidence suggests a still earlier date for established farming. Early forms of regular cultivation were apparently being practiced in the West African forestland during the middle centuries of the first millennium B.C., though not yet with iron tools. These early farmers in large part opened the way for all that was to follow.

Yet other folk joined them from time to time, settled down with them, intermarried with them, and combined with them in the making of new cultures and language variants. Where did these others come from? Many Ghana peoples have traditions which speak of origins elsewhere. Most of the Akan peoples believe that their forefathers came into Ghana from the north; and it was thanks to this tradition of "northern origin" that the founders of modern Ghana were able to name their country after the distant empire of the same name which flourished, a thousand years ago, in the westerly regions of the Western Sudan, and was known to medieval Arabs and Europeans as "the land of gold." The Ewe and the Ga, who have long lived in the southeastern part of Ghana, have traditions which say that their birthplace was in a country far toward the east, perhaps as far as the Lower Niger. The Nzima, for their part, trace their origin to lands which are now in the republics of Mali and Guinea.

Historians are inclined to believe that these "traditions of migration" contain a core of truth, but that the numbers who arrived were relatively small; perhaps they were no more than little bands of pioneers, under enterprising chiefs or practiced warriors, who were able to acquire new land and help to build new states. All of them, beyond any doubt, will have greatly intermingled with the peoples whom they found in occupation. And they will have done this perhaps as many as seven or eight centuries ago, so that they have long become fully indigenous to the land they live in now. In general, it may be said that all the peoples of Ghana have lived here since time immemorial.

This, of course, is not in the least to say that they have remained impervious to the passing years. On the contrary, Ghana has been the scene of social and economic development since the earliest times that historians can at present reach with any certainty, which means, in fact, the latter part of the fourteenth century. Thus the history of Ghana, in the sense of being a more or less understandable sequence of events and evolution, is about six hundred years old.

Much is known about the development of these six hundred years, and a good deal of what is known is helpful to a portrait of the Ghana of today. There is the singular case of the trade in gold.

In the Mediterranean world, up to about A.D. 900 or so, all major circuits of long-distance trade were based on the gold *denarius auri* of Byzantium. After that, with the eclipse of the Byzantine empire and the rise of the Fatimid empire centered on al-Kahira, or old Cairo, it was based on the gold *dinar* of the Arabs. Crucial to the maintenance of this North African *dinar* was the gold provided or minted by the traders of Morocco. This gold the Moroccans got by trade with the westerly regions of West Africa. Without West African gold, the monetary system of the medieval Mediterranean world could not have survived.

There was, of course, never enough. Fresh sources were sought. There came a new demand from Western Europe as the cities of Italy and Germany, and even the kings of England, acquired a prosperity they had not known before. At some time in the fourteenth century, the gold of central Ghana, of the forestlands of Asante and its neighbors, began to become an important element in the gold trade. This trade, northward to the Niger River and beyond the Niger across the Sahara to the Mediterranean, led to the founding of new states and trading cities. The old city of Timbuktu on the Middle Niger acquired large importance and, with neighboring Jenne a little further up the Niger, became a central entrepôt for the north-south trade. This was the "new trade" which enabled Western European kings and bankers to strike gold coins after many centuries of monetary debasement.

In exchange for their gold and other exports, the people of the forest country bought Mediterranean textiles and other manufactured goods, swords from Germany and Italy, and objects of luxury consumption. Some of these things survived for centuries, and a few of them are known even today. Perhaps the most impressive of these imported objects was a handled jug, or ewer, of English make which bears the badge of King Richard II, who reigned from 1377 to 1399; this was eventually looted by a British invading force near Kumase in 1896, and is now lodged in the British Museum. Long before they enjoyed any communication by way of the ocean, Ghana and northern Europe were in trading partnership by way of trans-Saharan intermediaries.

We know a little of the local states which drove this trade. The earliest of any importance was Bono, established on the northern fringes of the forest area in the fourteenth century. This state and its immediate neighbors undoubtedly contained an adequate force of mining labor that was skilled in methods of hand production, as well as in panning gold from rivers. These miners had already learned or invented, even at this early date, the techniques of tracing rock that contained the ores of gold, mining into this rock for a depth of fifty feet or more, crushing the ores with hand tools, and smelting them and working the residual metal. A modern estimate has suggested that by about A.D. 1500 these and other West African gold miners had produced a total of many hundred tons of gold. On this industrial enterprise, early states like Bono lived and throve.

Many different polities had emerged by that time, at least a dozen along the seaboard of what voyaging Europeans now began to call the Gold Coast, and far more than a dozen in the interior. As the prosperity of these populations grew by cultivation and by trade, so also did their size. With growing numbers there came new social and political problems. These reached a climax during the seventeenth and eighteenth centuries in a long and complex struggle for political and economic control. To all this, the traditions of Ghana bear eloquent witness. Here the pageant of history is starred with the names and feats of warriors and statesmen, prophets and rebels, and the intricate story of their triumphs or disasters.

Who should have mastery in the inland country where the gold was mined? Who should control the commerce with the Europeans in their forts along the seaboard? These were the prime questions, with the first far more important than the second. Gone were the days of the past when little communities could live in relative isolation without colliding with the interests of their neighbors. Centuries of slow but cumulative social and demographic growth had raised, in sixteenth-century Ghana, the same questions of power which occupied the Europe of that time. Often curiously reflected in the books and memoirs which visiting Europeans now began to write, great men and great events solidly emerge from historical inquiry.

The questions of who would control what were variously answered and settled, though not quickly. For more than two confused centuries there was a baffling and many-sided effort, by one state after another, to secure mastery over a wide area of the forestland or its neighboring seaboard. Not until the beginning of the eighteenth century did a single great power—that of the Akan state of Asante, or Ashanti as Europeans have generally pronounced and written the name—prove capable of asserting a clear ascendancy, and of keeping it. Before that the center of the stage was held by two other Akan states, Denkyira and Akwamu, the former being active in the western forestland and the latter mainly near the coast.

These two states have long since vanished from the scene, but the Europeans of those days knew them well—if only because European trading forts along the Gold Coast seaboard were largely dependent on Denkyira and Akwamu for success with the inland trade. Akwamu took shape in the ambitions of a people living not far inland from Accra. Under an energetic king called Ansa Sasraku, they set out in 1670 to carve an empire for themselves. First, they subdued some of their smaller neighbors. Then, they overcame the Ga people of Accra and nearby coastal towns. Next, they asserted their overlordship upon the Fante to the west, and over the Ewe and others to the east.

Eventually, they exercised hegemony along the whole seaboard from about modern Cape Coast to the old ports of the Slave Coast, which afterwards became part of Dahomey. Yet their success was brief. Based on no sufficient principle of central authority, the Akwamu empire began to fall apart in 1710 and by 1731 had disappeared.

Denkyira's story was after the same style. Also an Akan people, the Denkyira gained control over the western forest country in the early part of the seventeenth century. They brought within their tribute-exacting overlordship most of the smaller clans or sections of their neighborhood, together with some of the chief sources of Ghanaian gold. They struck up good relations with the Dutch merchants who had now ousted the Portuguese from the castle of Elmina, which the Portuguese had built as long ago as 1482. With all this, Denkyira prospered from exploitation of a trading cycle which involved the export of gold and other goods in exchange for the import of European manufacturers, not the least important of which, by this time, were firearms and gunpowder.

The Denkyira, like their rivals and successors, were the masters in this trade. Not for another two centuries would Europeans along the coast be more than junior trading partners or auxiliaries. This is an historical fact which helps to explain the general confidence and self-esteem of the Ghanaian temperament, an aspect that was scarcely altered by the invasions and subjections of the colonial period. Anyone who wanders about Ghana today will soon notice it. More than in many countries, a man in Ghana is likely to be admired according to his merits, or at least according to his claims, but certainly not according to the color of his skin. Some Europeans and Americans have disliked this; others, and no doubt the majority, have found in it the basis for friendship.

When the Portuguese had first appeared on this coast, five hundred years ago, they claimed a right of monopoly over and against all other Europeans by virtue of a papal dispensation. But the English and the French, and afterwards the Dutch, the Prussians, and the Swedes and Danes, soon made an end to any such pretensions. They came in peacefully if they could, but by warfare on the Portuguese if they must. There were many inter-European clashes. Watching these quarrels, Africans along the seaboard quickly found their own advantage in playing off one European nation against another.

Akwamu and Denkyira both illustrate this situation. The conquering king of Akwamu found the English and the Danes in Accra. He proceeded to trade with both of them. But in 1694 the local Danish governor fell into dispute with the king's representatives, thinking, no doubt, that he was strong enough in his castle of Christiansborg to call whatever trading tune he pleased. But the Akwamu, then at the height of their power, thought otherwise. They mounted a surprise attack and, in the words of a contemporary English observer, "forced the Danes' general to fly to the Dutch to save his life."

Yet war on the Danes was by no means war on other Europeans. The Akwamu needed trade, and were concerned only with keeping their partners in order. While they established themselves in Christiansborg Castle and for the better part of a year flew from its battlements their own flag, an African brandishing a sword upon a field of white, they extended their trading links with the English. An English captain who dined with the Akwamu governor of Christiansborg in that year of 1694 found during dinner that the governor "drank the King of England's, the [English] African Company's and our own healths frequently, with volleys of cannon. . . ."

But to keep the Danes permanently out of Christiansborg would have been to favor a local English monopoly. The Akwamu had no interest in doing that. About a year after they had seized the castle, they accordingly handed it back to the repentant Danes in exchange for a handsome compensation which the Danes were obliged to pay in gold.

Westward along the coast the situation of the Dutch at Elmina Castle, which they had taken from the Portuguese by force of arms in 1637, was not much different in relation to the Denkyira. Like the Portuguese before them, the Dutch paid rent for the land on which the castle stood, and the landlords, by this time, were the Denkyira. As good tenants, the Dutch found themselves expected to support the interests of the Denkyira against neighboring rivals.

These rivals were mainly the Fante, who, in turn, also had "their Europeans" in the shape of the English at Cape Coast Castle. Often bitterly at odds in Europe, the English and the Dutch now found themselves on different sides in the Gold Coast. The situation, in short, was one of mutual advantage as between Africans and Europeans, but with the Africans holding the upper hand. For if the Denkyira and the Fante, like the Akwamu, depended in no small degree on the good will of their respective European partners, especially when firearms became important in warfare after about 1650, the Europeans on their side were in a still more dependent position. Weak and far from home, they were able to conduct this trading system only by careful diplomacy and an acceptance of African sovereignty.

Akwamu disintegrated after 1730, beset by rivals and internal conflicts which it could not master. But forty years earlier, northwestward in the forest country, another power had begun to make its influence felt. While England was celebrating her Glorious Revolution of 1688, and putting down foundations for a later maritime supremacy, another kind of revolution was occurring in the groves and clearings of Asante, and here too there were the beginnings of a powerful state. Its origins were in several Akan groups who had lately prospered from a share in the gold trade and from their skill in forest farming. For many years these groups had fallen within the sphere of Denkyira, to which they were obliged to pay an annual tribute in gold and labor. Now they too set forth upon a quest for overlordship. In this, they were to succeed far better than any of their neighbors.

Out of their efforts came the memorable kingdom of Asante; and Asante would dominate or profoundly influence the whole life and land of what is modern Ghana for nearly two centuries. Further, with the development of Asante there arose a pattern of inner political conflict which was to survive after this kingdom had finally met defeat at the hands of British invaders. Even the politics of independence, after 1957, was to show this pattern repeatedly. It was a pattern of intra-ethnic rivalry that we might call national rivalry. Along the coast and in the plains behind the coast were the states of the southern Akan, of the Fante and their neighbors, and those of non-Akan peoples such as the Ga and Ewe. By the seventeenth century, these had become integral parts of the European maritime trade, under the leadership of one or another of the European trading powers, and were its principal intermediaries with the trade of the inland country.

The central country, after 1700, was ruled by the Asante. They had a dual interest in the long-distance trade, northward to the Niger and the Saharan intermediaries, and southward to the coast and the Europeans. Their kings prosecuted both interests by a considered strategy of conquest. Little by little, they brought the northern plains under their control, leaving the states intact but making them subject to Asante overlordship. And they did the same, if not easily, with the southern states along the coast. But the southern states never accepted this overlordship with anything save great reluctance, and eventually saw their salvation in making an alliance with the British.

The foundations of Asante have the vivid quality of heroic legend. Gradually, its leading groups learned to work together. Already in the 1650's they had moved toward a loose confederation which could at least avert internal disputes and strengthen each group against Denkyira, their overlord, and against their rivals in the north, the Domaa, and in the south, the Akim. At this point, there appeared on the scene one of those founder-heroes in which the oral history of tropical Africa so frequently abounds. This man was Osei Tutu. He it was, renowned in war and respected for his statesmanship, who transformed the loose confederacy which he found into the Asante Union, and organized a nation.

In this, however, Osei Tutu was not alone. Guiding and advising him was another celebrated figure, *Okomfo* Anokye, the Priest Anokye, who devised and carried through the actual work of union. This he did, essentially, by finding ways of asserting the supremacy of one line of ancestors over all the separate lines to which the several groups paid homage. Up to that time, the situation in this part of the forest country could be compared with that of the warring principalities or states of ancient Greece. United in one nation, these Greek states could have spared themselves internecine warfare and avoided disasters from outside. But they were never able to unite. With the Akan states of the central forest area, it was different. The Asante leaders succeeded where the Athenians stopped short.

By about 1695 (this date is no more than approximate), Osei Tutu and *Okomfo* Anokye were ready to act. The leaders of the various large lineage-groups were called together in assembly. And at this assembly, after suitable preparations, Anokye "in the presence of a great multitude"—to quote the version collected by an Englishman half a century ago—and "with the help of his supernatural power, is stated to have brought down from the sky, in a black cloud, and amid rumblings, and in air thick with white dust, a wooden stool with three supports and partly covered with gold. . . .This stool did not fall to earth but alighted slowly upon Osei Tutu's knees. . . .And Anokye told Osei Tutu and all the people that this stool contained the *sunsum* [soul, or spirit] of the Asante nation, and that their power, their health, their bravery, their welfare were in this stool . . . and that if this stool were taken or destroyed, then, just as a man sickens and dies whose *sunsum* . . . has wandered away or has been injured . . . so would the Asante nation sicken and lose its vitality and power."

It can have been no mere caprice that the sacred stool should have been made with gold. Without a firm command of the gold trade the wealth of Ashanti would undoubtedly sicken and die, so that one may perhaps compare this sacred Golden Stool with the corporation badge of some great trading company. However that may be, and the traditions of course say nothing of the kind, the Golden Stool became a potent symbol of unity and strength. Speaking in its name, or rather in the name of the spiritual and ancestral power for which it stood, Osei Tutu the Asantehene, the king of this new nation, enacted laws by which it became a grievous crime to recite the separate political traditions of the groups that were now joined in the Union. Henceforward, all these groups were to regard themselves as a single people.

Once forged, this union held firm. Based on it, energetic kings threw off the overlordship of Denkyira and brought one after another of their neighbors under their own hegemony. Soon they had taken over direct trading relations with the Dutch at Elmina; and during the eighteenth century their power radiated across the land of modern Ghana, as well as parts of northern Ghana, the Ivory Coast, and Togo.

They collided briefly with the English in 1806. Here again one may glimpse the true nature of the European-African relationship before colonial times. The armies of the Asantehene clashed with the English because the English showed signs of giving active support to the Fante, partners of the English at Cape Coast and nearby, whereas the Asante claimed the Fante as their own vassals by right of conquest. But the clash was brief, and peace was soon restored. Not until sixty-eight years later would Britain, now launched upon imperial enterprise, move in from the coast with armies bent on violent invasion; and even so, it was not until 1900 that the power of Asante would be finally destroyed.

Defeat flowed, once again, from technological inferiority. Traditional African civilization could not make those scientific and economic transformations which enabled Europe to assert its colonial supremacy in Africa. While several African states, with Asante perhaps the most successful among them, had indeed developed an impressive flexibility and strength of internal organization, they had not crossed the great industrial divide. They remained in an age before machine production and all that this implied.

Yet the local achievement was by no means small. One can measure this achievement in several ways. Although they ruled over a largely nonliterate society, the Asante kings well understood the values of literacy. Without accepting Islam, they nonetheless welcomed literate Muslims from the Western Sudan and gave them positions of influence in the organization of trade and the management of royal affairs. By the middle of the nineteenth century, the Asante monarch was perfectly capable of conducting a written correspondence, through Muslim chancery clerks, with any of his several neighbors who were able to do the same.

Moreover, absence of wheeled transport—and horses, in any case, could not be bred in Asante nor

easily kept there, even for short periods—did not spell bad communications. On the contrary, the Asante rulers disposed of an excellent system of radial foot-roads. "The king knows each day what is happening in the most humble villages of his empire," a Frenchman in Asante service could write in the 1870's. "From all sides he receives reports and minute details. . . .Conversely, day and night, the orders of the king are despatched in all directions. . . ." This king "is one of the busiest men that one could see," having authority and using it over questions of "war, religion, commerce, agriculture, weights-and-measures, price and tariffs of all kinds, and finally of the exercise of justice, which is not the least of his responsibilities."

These advances reflected a general shift in political system and organization among many African states. As in other dynamic polities, whether African or not, the gradual expansion of civilization carried with it a steady pressure for the strengthening of central power. This was a time when the old and venerable divisions of society into groups descended from different lines of ancestors—what we may call vertical divisions of society—were increasingly complicated and modified by new kinds of division, horizontal division, which saw the rise of men of wealth and power at one end of the scale, and the extension of bonded or servile labor among peasants at the other.

In Africa, these horizontal divisions never acquired the sharp rigidities and consequences of class divisions in Europe; but history was now increasingly made by the elevation of one section of the community at the expense of other sections, and especially of ordinary peasants who were forced into captive labor. By the second half of the nineteenth century, the kings of Asante had developed a state bureaucracy under their personal command, had raised a full-time mercenary fighting corps, and had begun to substitute the old loyalties of vassalage for new loyalties of direct obedience through governors and sub-governors. Their position and powers were now in some ways comparable with those of the royal governments of pre-revolutionary Europe.

Yet there were big differences. Asante knew no expropriation of land in favor of royal ownership, and, in other than an embryonic sense, horizontal divisions did not become class divisions. Thus there remained a large measure of traditional democracy, and the acerbities of royal power were continually checked by popular controls. This "democratic spirit" of pre-colonial Africa was more than a mere legend. It governed the behavior of rulers and operated in a manner that was far more tolerant and egalitarian than anything known in England before the revolution of 1642, in France before that of 1789, or in Russia before that of 1917.

Earlier Europeans had seen this truth, though they were able only faintly to describe it. Writing of Fante government in the 1840's, a Scots observer named Brodie Cruickshank commented that "it was not a despotism, not a constitutional monarchy, nor an oligarchy, nor a republic, but partook of something of the qualities of each of these different forms, and depended much upon the individual character and riches of the chief. It was, moreover, greatly modified by traditional customs and precedents, which appear to define the extent of the chiefs' authority, as well as the privileges of the people, and to be equally binding on both. . . ."

Later and more scientific inquiry has expanded this shrewd if rather puzzled observation. We know now that the power of chiefs was generally hedged about with checks and balances against the abuse or persistent failure of authority; and that while the rights of the individual often left much to be desired, in point of democratic freedom, the obligations of the community were as often shaped to protect the individual's welfare and status.

And this was so not only among the go-ahead peoples of the forest and coastal country. Emphatic ideas about the proper standing of rights and duties as between individual and community were an inseparable part of all these old systems, and were regularly translated into institutions designed to safeguard the one and the other. The peoples of the north were no exception. Those who lived in thatch-and-clay grassland villages (such as Strand so evocatively shows us here) were also embraced in cultures of this kind. These northern peoples, the Tallensi, Konkomba and others, lived not by chance or chaos, but within close-knit patterns of social rights and duties. These patterns have revealed a consistent allowance for individual liberty and error within societies of great stability.

Such "village polities" could well appear primitive to outsiders. When British administrative officers first took authority over the Tallensi, back in 1911, they found no chiefs or governments through whom they could exercise their new colonial rule. The Tallensi of these villages, as Meyer Fortes tells us, had "no indigenous political institutions of the type we associate with centralised government." They had no policemen, courts of law, political assemblies, or any other of the paraphernalia of organized social power. And yet they did not live without law and order. Their system composed a balance of rules and regulations, well understood by the Tallensi if not by the British, whereby crime was condemned and punished, wars were prevented or else kept small and short, morals were supervised with a pointed peasant realism, and the good of the community generally upheld against individual backslidings and temptations.

Little of this was recognized by the confident arbiters of colonial authority. One may still usefully remember that the word "native" became synonymous not with what it really meant, but with the infantile and second-rate. This irritated Ghanaian intellectuals, but it also made them laugh. Having argued a legal case in 1906, J. Mensah Sarbah, one of Ghana's early spokesmen (there is now a residence hall of Ghana University named after him), recalled how he had questioned a European mining expert. "After [this expert] had spoken of *native* bush-path, *native* canoe, *native* river, *native* mines and *native* gold, I asked him to explain to the Court, in what respects *native* gold and *native* things particularly differed from those found in other parts of the world, but he could not; for the absurdity of always describing in Africa everything non-European as *native* had dawned on him by that time."

During those early days of colonial rule in Africa, many ideas would be minted that were later to become the common coin of African political argument and thought. In the 1950's, for example, the ideas of *négritude*, of Negro-ness, were to be famously sung by the poets and used by the politicians. Sometimes they acquired a racist undertone. But not in Ghana. Here they were used as verbal gateways to the ideas of a common humanity up and down the world. So much may be seen in the well-known simile of another forerunner, the educationalist J. E. K. Aggrey, when he said that the music of humanity could be compared with the notes of a piano: neither the black keys nor the white keys could be omitted. Or consider this other saying of Aggrey's: "If I went to Heaven and God said: 'Aggrey, I am going to send you back, would you like to go as a white man?' I should reply, 'No, send me back as a black man, yes, completely black.' And if God should ask 'Why?' I would reply, 'Because I have a work to do as a black man that no white man can do. Please send me back as black as you can make me. . . .I am proud of my colour: whoever is not proud of his colour is not fit to live.'"

All this belonged to the ideological struggles of the outright colonial period and its aftermath. But it drew some of its emotive strength, in one way or another, from the consequences of a further aspect of the pre-colonial history of Ghana as of other West African lands. This was the slave trade to the Americas, with everything that this implied for the making of "world opinion." Strand's faithful portrait gives us its hint of that as well: of the castles and the dungeons, the darkness and the sorrow.

FOUR FROM GOLD TO SLAVES

It would be said long afterwards, when the leading nationalist party of modern Ghana, the Convention People's Party, had duly come to power in 1957, that the country was ruled above all by the interests of Ghana's traders, and that their interests turned generally on short-term calculations of profit and loss to the individuals who commanded political power. There is much to support this comment. The history of Ghana shows that one need not be surprised.

The interests, for example, of the great Asante kingdom and its monarchs were multifarious, but considerations of trade were always predominant. The accumulation of wealth was seen as a positive good. "The Asante view of the position of the individual within society, as trustee of the legacy of the ancestors on behalf of the generations yet unborn," we are told by Ivor Wilks, the historian of Asante, "carried the implication that the good citizen was the one who worked to bequeath more to his successors than he had acquired from his predecessors." The accumulation should be social in that ideally it should be intended to benefit a given group or community or nation; but the individual should nonetheless be active in making it.

The Fante and other coastal peoples thought the same, except that here, along the coast as distinct from Asante, there was much scope for the rise of independent traders who were not, at least in their origins, "kings and great men" as the Asante king Osei Bonsu called them. By the seventeenth century, the oversea trade with Europeans had begun to give rise to what a Ghanaian historian, Kwame Yeboa Daaku, has called "a new class of middlemen." These merchant adventurers of the coast became wealthy. And as they became wealthy they also became powerful. There was John Claessen, who after 1656 controlled a fleet of war canoes and as many as two thousand musketeers. There was Asomani of Akwamu, who seized Christiansborg Castle from the Danes in 1693. There was John Kabes, whose local power was formidable in the 1680's. And there was John Konny, who defeated an Anglo-Dutch alliance mounted against him and, after 1711, "commanded by far and away the largest force of any single power on the coast."

The energy and independence of these great traders built and conserved their fortunes. The Europeans had often to play second fiddle among them.

But relative European weakness on the spot

concealed an inner strength which always, in the end, gave Europeans the upper hand. For they alone held the sea and thus the access to markets that lay beyond it. Out of this came African involvement in the Atlantic slave trade.

At least by 1650, the Europeans' demand for captives who could be sold into plantation slavery across the Atlantic had become a prime factor in all their trade with Africa. Why did Africa's "kings and great men" not only accept this slave trade but powerfully work to enlarge it? All question of contemporary morality apart, the broad answers appear to run something like this. First, the maritime trade (like the trans-Saharan trade before it) had become a vital component in the political and economic calculations of African kings and men of substance. Second, the Europeans wanted captives more than they wanted anything else: as time went by, they wanted captives even more than they wanted gold. Investing in captives who could be sold as slaves had become very good business—on both sides of the bargain.

Third, and perhaps decisively, the structures of West African society provided an already existing basis onto which the trade in captives could be grafted. Though in many ways already a mercantile economy, that of West Africa was not yet a fully monetary one, far less a capitalist one. Labor in important sectors was performed by slaves who received no wages in the common sense of the term. But "slaves" is a misnomer if we apply it in the familiar trans-Atlantic sense of plantation slavery. The men and women who provided this "wageless labor" were people who had lost their civic rights through such means as conquest or capture in war or sentence of the courts. That being the case, they were fitted into society by being taken into this or that lineage group or extended family upon condition that they worked for their keep. In this way, they acquired certain valuable rights—among them, the right to marry their masters' daughters or inherit their masters' property, or set up in trade of their own. On the other hand, they remained "disposable." They could be bought and sold. They could be moved from one servitude to another.

While historians are not altogether agreed upon these matters, there seems rather little doubt that the origins of African participation in the Atlantic slave trade (as with the earlier and less destructive trans-Saharan slave trade) lay in the exchange of "wageless laborers"—invariably called "slaves" in the European records—for imported goods. The next component in the chain of cause and effect was the possibility of buying firearms and gunpowder. These, almost from the first, were rightly seen by African rulers as a means of increasing their political power. But by this time the European demand for slaves had become far in excess of the number of "disposable" persons available within any given society. To sustain the trade with Europeans, it was therefore necessary to acquire more. The acquisition was achieved through warfare. So that by about 1700 the great majority of slaves being taken from Africa were in no real sense slaves; they were prisoners made in wars waged to capture them. That was one large reason why John Claessen, for example, needed his two thousand musketeers, and John Konny his "largest force of any single power on the coast."

The Asante kings of the inland country also went into the slave trade, and for the same reasons. They could sustain or extend their power only if they could be assured of arms and powder. But to obtain these it was no longer enough to sell gold; now they also had to sell captives. Of such captives they assured themselves of a sufficient quantity, year by year, through raiding or purchase in the northern territories. Like other African kings, or like the European kings of the Middle Ages, they seldom sold their own citizens (when they did, it was chiefly to get rid of this or that criminal or political rebel). They captured the citizens of their neighbors, and sold them.

In this way, the slave trade began and grew, thrusting its pitiless fingers into country after country, until there was scarcely a polity in Western Africa that was not providing, through its neighbors, a quota of captives for the mines and plantations of the Americas. Most of the ancestors of black Americans came from those countries of Western Africa lying between Senegal in the far northwest and Angola in the far southwest. Nearly all, after about 1500, were sold by neighboring African peoples, although enterprising

European traders now and then mounted slaving expeditions of their own.

Ghana, as it happens, was not a particularly large exporter of captives. This was partly because the coastal states could and did defend their citizens from the magnitude of slaving disasters which befell some other lands, such as Angola. Partly, too, it was because the rulers of Asante had their own large domestic need of "wageless labor," whether for gold production or porterage along the roads of their kingdom. There were even times, indeed, when Europeans had to bring gold to the Gold Coast in order to obtain captives. Some recent studies by Philip Curtin, for example, show that only about one-tenth of all captives imported during the eighteenth century into Jamaica, into the great French sugar colony of Saint Domingue (afterwards Haiti), and into the United States were from Ghana. And not all of these will have been from Ghana itself; many came from further north.

But Ghana had another kind of importance for the trade. Here, along the seaboard, stood a notable concentration of European trading posts and forts. The Portuguese had built the first of these at Elmina in 1482. They had been joined by the English and the Dutch, the Danes and Swedes and Prussians, so that, by the nineteenth century, such forts or castles numbered more than forty. So far as the slave trade was concerned, they were particularly important as gathering-points and "warehouses" for captives brought by sea from elsewhere.

Some of these castles remain more or less intact, and one or two are still habitable or have been restored for habitation by a Ghana government interested in attracting tourists. Several have a striking architectural beauty that nonetheless conserves, within their high white walls, a strong atmosphere of the bitterness over which they reigned. Huddled in these castles, their lives desperately shortened by the fevers that no one understood, European governors and agents dealt in the export-import trade with many items on either side, but always with captives who passed through their cells and slave marts.

All that, for the most part, was already in the past a hundred years ago. Yet the legacy of the trade in captives remained even when, at last, the trade itself was stopped. In America, the legacy of slavery was to be the condition of black Americans; in Africa, it was to be the colonial period.

Just as the old "legitimate" trade of the sixteenth century, when the sale and purchase of captives was practiced only by the Portuguese, had built in time a maritime commercial system which led on to the vast Atlantic slave trade of later years, so did this slave trade lead on to colonial invasion. The ways in which it did this were various. Imperialist rivalries within Western Europe also played their part after the 1870's. In any case, the domination of the African coastal trade by Europeans with a rapidly increasing technological superiority became a large factor in weakening African ability to resist invasion. And then, of course, there were local factors which helped European encroachment: in the example of Ghana, as we have seen, the desire of coastal peoples to use the Europeans, by this time only the British, as a means of warding off or diminishing the claims of Asante.

FIVE THE MODEL COLONY

The outright colonial period in southern Ghana may be said to have begun in the 1860's, in Asante in 1900, and a little later in the savanna lands to the north of Asante; and for all of these the period of colonial rule came to an end in 1957. In the long run of history, this is not very long; moreover, the impact of colonial rule at least in West Africa was often superficial. This is one reason why modern African historians are inclined to regard colonial rule as an episode rather than a major interruption marking the end of one "era" and the onset of another.

There is much to be said for this view of the colonial period in West Africa, though less when considering other parts of the colonized continent, and least of all when taking into account the colonial impact in countries settled by large numbers of whites. West Africa was relatively fortunate in this respect. For a number of reasons, including the malarial mosquito and the efficacy of African resistance to white settlement, only one or two West African countries were ever regarded as suitable for permanent occupation by whites, and Ghana was not among these. Without white settlement, the "colonial equation" resolved itself into a more or less simple opposition of British imperial interests and local African interests. Though influenced by the British presence in the fields of trade and European education, the people of Ghana were perfectly able to conserve their own culture, even if they were unable to develop it. It needs only the briefest sojourn in Ghana to understand that this culture has remained quite largely intact.

Yet this does not mean that the colonial period was nothing more than an exasperating period for peoples who could never be in any doubt about their ability to rule themselves. The exasperation was often very great, and sometimes unbearable. Especially in the economic field, it led to an increasing distortion of the country's capacity to produce wealth, fitting this capacity more and more restrictively into the overall imperial system. The fact remains, however, that all the major trends that were to surface after the colonial period had come to an end, in 1957, were at least potentially if not actually present in the pre-colonial period.

While not forgetting the subjective aspects of the matter, whether of exasperation at being ruled by foreigners or of humiliation at having to accept that rule, one can look at the whole period from a number of objective angles. Once again, these are above all commercial angles.

The Asante offer a useful case history. By the early decades of the nineteenth century, the trade of this strong kingdom had grown to a point at which some emphatically modernizing trends had begun to appear. These were especially associated with King Osei Bonsu, who reigned during the first decades of that century. He improved the administration, added new departments ("stools"), and greatly enlarged the number of persons—the *batafo*—who were licensed as agents entitled to carry on the king's trade, partly to their personal advantage.

After the defeat of 1874, when the Asante army was shattered by a large British force including auxiliary troops from southern Ghana, there set in something of a reaction against the Asante king's all-pervasive control of trade. This was associated with that growing class of men—the *asikafo*, or "rich men" —who had made money out of land or farming, and now desired a chance to trade on their own. State control in fact was reasserted, but the rulers now knew enough about the British and their capacities to see that a further large dose of modernization could still be wise, and perhaps altogether necessary.

There emerged the idea of what Ivor Wilks has called a "neo-mercantilism": that is, the association of Asante state power with British or other European capital in a program of development that would exclude private enterprise. If it was necessary to come to terms with the British, as obviously it was after the military defeat of 1874, then perhaps it had better be by way of this kind of "partnership in development." If railways were now seen to be desirable, then who but the British could and would build them in Asante? The answer might well be an economic alliance between oversea investors and the state, thus greatly extending the old "mercantile" system of the eighteenth century. So far did this desire for alliance go, if admittedly under threat of renewed British invasion, that the Asante rulers brought themselves in 1895 to offer the British the right to establish a chartered company. This company in Asante was to have "the same extensive rights as at present enjoyed by the British South Africa Company" in the lands which that company was then invading in southern Africa, the lands that became the colonies of Southern and Northern Rhodesia.

How far such concessions might have gone in practice is another matter. Like the British Royal Niger Company in Nigeria, the British South Africa Company included local sovereignty in the assumptions of its operation. Whether or not it set about "modernizing" the Rhodesias could no doubt be a matter for argument: what is certain is that it began this task by entirely dispossessing the Africans of Southern Rhodesia, and by treating those of Northern Rhodesia as customers for the same recipe. In any case, the Asante offer was rejected. By 1895 the British imperial government wanted outright possession for its own sake, or in order to forestall the French, who, it was reasonably feared, nourished ambitions of the same kind. British invasion duly followed, and Asante was formally annexed in 1901.

Two points of long importance emerge at this juncture. The first is that European civilization now began to be made, in educated African opinion, the equivalent of modernization. Without the first, it would be said, there could be none of the second; and this thought would echo down all the colonial years and for long after. It placed the educated intellectuals in their characteristic dilemma. They wished on one side to advance the cause of their people and their culture. On the other side they became deeply convinced that this could be done only by a process of "Europeanization."

Attoh Ahuma was an example of those Gold Coast intellectuals who spoke most vehemently and eloquently for the virtues of their people and culture. But he also thought that they must be "civilized" by the adoption of European ideas and modes—of what would shortly become the "European model," here in the Gold Coast seen in its British form. "Let us help one another to find a way out of Darkest Africa," he wrote in 1911. "The impenetrable jungle around us is not darker than the dark primeval forest of the human mind uncultured. . . .We must emerge from the savage backwoods and come into the open where nations are made." This was a whole political program. The intellectuals would pursue it for decades into the future.

A second point is that the modernization of Asante, its economic and social development from the condition of the nineteenth century, could also appear as perfectly consonant with a partnership in which European capital and know-how would play the dominant and locally privileged role. Here again was

another thought that would long survive, and survives even now in the face of some very powerful and painful evidence to the contrary. Nkrumah would adopt it as his own at least until the early 1960's. His successors would see it as the only right and proper policy, even though, by their time, other Africans would denounce any such partnership as only another form of colonial rule.

Thus the groundwork for all the major policies of the post-colonial period were generally in place, if still at an elementary stage of understanding, even before the British took over.

The same was true, in other ways, along the coast. The "new class of African middlemen" of the seventeenth century was duly followed by many others, so that the history of coastal trade during the nineteenth century was above all one of African enterprise. After 1900, with the growth of major monopolist firms such as the British United Africa Company, an offshoot of the Unilever combine, the big African traders along the coast were squeezed out of business and vanished from the scene. But they were not forgotten. After independence, their memory returned with a new force, for now there were fresh opportunities available to African businessmen. These opportunities occurred, true enough, in a situation that no longer favored or even permitted the emergence of an African capitalist class. But they were eagerly seized, at whatever level they might offer, by new traders who, using the political influence of the nationalist movement, quickly gave Nkrumah's party its deeply commercial nature.

Beyond joining the goal of modernization to European thought and European capital, there was a third way in which the trading system of the pre-colonial years would shape the colony that the British ruled. New forms of export goods were discovered. Exports of natural rubber enjoyed a brief prosperity. But then came cocoa. Introduced by Ghanaian initiative in the 1890's, cocoa rapidly boomed. During the colonial period it became Ghana's major export, practically a monoculture, and Ghana became the greatest cocoa exporter in the world. Yet in building this achievement the colonial rulers had almost no part at all, while their monopolist trading companies, after a brief and futile effort to produce cocoa for themselves, became content merely to buy the cocoa when it reached the coast, caring only that they bought it for as little as possible. There is a large sense in which the history of the colonial period in Ghana was written in cocoa. And the writing was Ghanaian, not British. Adjusting to the situation and to new techniques of operation, Ghanaians moved into cocoa production with a skill and drive which are only now beginning to be measured at their true value. What they were doing, essentially, was simply extending the export-import system of pre-colonial times, even if the terms of trade might sorely go against them now.

In all these ways it may be said that the colonial period really was a continuation, episodical or not, rather than a major point of change, in the working out or enlargement of underlying trends already in existence. And this goes a long way to explain why Ghana (then known as the Gold Coast Colony and Protectorate) became what the British enjoyed calling a "model colony" and, content to be led by Ghanaians who equated modernization with the teachings of the civilization of Western Europe, gave little more than verbal trouble at least until the 1940's. If Ghanaians found the British to be satisfactory on the whole, even though continually exasperating and not seldom humiliating, this again would be because their basic attitudes were in tune with the kinds of enterprise which the British favored.

Much the same might be said of a number of other West African colonies, and certainly of southern Nigeria. Yet there was still another reason, here in Ghana, for the relative ease with which the leading elements on the two "sides," the African and the British, proved able to accommodate to each other. This was that the process of colonial enclosure—the dispossession of African sovereignty, the transformation of alliance into subjection or partnership into servitude—was a very gradual one. There was here no rapid gulping down of vast anonymous regions such as occurred in some other regions. The take-over was slow and hesitant. The British had required many years to establish their effective supremacy along the coast. And when this supremacy was finally "real-

ized," during the 1850's or a little later, it had long acquired a certain air of naturalness for the peoples of the coast. The British, after all, were useful to these peoples: not only as trading partners, but increasingly as allies against the power of Asante.

The British had brushed with Asante as early as 1806. This skirmish led to nothing further, and peace returned. What was required, clearly, was a mutually advantageous working relationship; and British emissaries duly paid their respects at the court of the king of Asante as early as 1817. Not unnaturally, the coastal allies of the British saw things differently. If the British were going to prefer Asante to themselves, then half—perhaps more—of the value of their own "European connection" must be lost.

On the British side, moreover, there was also by this time an "imperial factor" concerned with Africa: still fairly low in key, operating from an economic and military base that was comparatively weak, working on a metropolitan opinion far more preoccupied with India and America, yet present on the scene and capable of influence. In imperial London, as in other countries that collected colonies, a feeling was emerging that European prestige must insist on African defeat. The great Victorian century would steadily inflame and infuriate this racist conviction.

Even so, the process was erratic. In 1824 a mixed British and African force under the command of Sir Charles Macarthy, the British coastal governor, was cut to pieces by an Asante army on the Bonsa River; badly wounded, Macarthy killed himself rather than be captured. Two years later the Asante, in their turn, were sorely beaten at Dodowa, not far from Accra, by another mixed force under British command. All this, of course, was not yet the imperialism of later decades. Back in Kumase there were those who thought that the British could be well enough contained by a skillful diplomacy of peace. Back in London, there were those who thought the same in reverse. No effort was made to exploit the victory at Dodowa; on the contrary, the troops were ordered to return to the coast. More than that, the London government even saw the victory as a convenient prelude to complete withdrawal of British official power. Now that they had defeated the Asante in fair fight, who could accuse them of running away? In 1828, accordingly, a British warship was sent to evacuate private merchants and their property, while its captain carried orders instructing the British commander to destroy his forts and retire by sea to Sierra Leone.

But if not yet the century of imperialism in Africa, this was already the century of thrusting merchant enterprise there. The British traders on the coast were opposed to cutting their losses; they objected to withdrawal; they did not want to be evacuated. Their Fante friends and partners naturally supported them. For what would happen to them if the British packed their bags and went?

A compromise was reached. The British government withdrew. But London also agreed to underwrite, at the rate of £4,000 a year, a sort of merchants' government in the two settlements of Accra and Cape Coast. These were to be ruled by an elected council and an English governor: a rather characteristically pragmatic device, one may think, whereby it was hoped to cut the loss but keep the profit. There was a clear hope in London that the affairs of the Gold Coast, a distant place of which London knew little and cared less, could thus be settled for a long time to come. Yet London reckoned without the times and their underlying drive: in particular, without the accident of Captain George Maclean.

Maclean was the first governor under this new dispensation. Coming ashore in 1830, he soon won a name for skill and good sense. A crucial point, once again, was that the Fante found it convenient to have the British on the spot. Together with Maclean's "forward policy," this attitude soon put a new complexion on affairs. In 1844, with further developments, there came the famous "Bond." By this document, eight Fante and neighboring rulers voluntarily recognized the legality of British administration along the coast. Two consequences followed: on the one hand, the limit of British power was defined, with the local rulers conferring no rights of sovereignty or even of suzerainty, and affirming their independence; on the other hand, they admitted the legality of British presence, and this was to become the foundation for every future British encroachment.

In itself, this "Bond" and its immediate impli-cations did rather little. One can say that it merely regularized a *de facto* position which all had long accepted. But by this time there was another factor on the scene, even if the Fante rulers did not see it—and even if the British themselves were scarcely aware of it. This new factor was the growing and imperious force of a European nationalism translated, or in the course of being translated, into territorial expansion overseas.

Many reasons may be adduced for the great imperial adventure in Africa: Anglo-French rivalry or other such conflicts that clamored on the scene as Britannia's claim to rule the waves, and more than the waves, was increasingly contested; the pressures of local trading interest concerned with retaining or achieving local monopolies on this or that part of the African coast; the influence of missionaries convinced of Europe's duty to "conquer barbarism by Christianity and Commerce"; the accident of soldiers and adventurers on the make. All these and other motives were part of the story behind "the Scramble for Africa," or what a notable French imperialist of the 1880's, Jules Ferry, would call "this immense steeple-chase into the unknown." But all such reasons, however valid in themselves, were incidental. The scenario they made was *Hamlet* without the Dane, or at least without his father's ghost.

The central actor, the real motivating force, the ghostly presence: this was something else. Crudely put, this was the expansive nature of European capitalism. One may argue learnedly about the economic requirements or consequences of that nature—about how far, for instance, this imperialism was ever powered (save in South Africa) by any mere need to find new outlets for "investible surplus." All I wish to do here is to focus on its cultural nature, using the term "cultural" to cover all those beliefs and attitudes, hopes, fears, hatreds and assembled horrors that repeatedly steered the policies of the leading European powers after about 1870, conceived and carried through the occupation of the whole of Africa, and led eventually to the lunatic holocausts of the First World War.

Nothing less than this imbrication of "cultural factors" can explain the sheer gratuitousness of the "Scramble." Huge territories were occupied simply for the sake of "the flag." Wars were waged which can now make no sense to rational men—and which made no sense, as one could easily show, to the rational men of that time. What could have better suited the onward expansion of the British economy than the right to establish a chartered company in Asante? Yet the British imperialists of the 1890's would not have it. They wanted conquest: in itself and for itself, quite aside from any lesser influence they might feel in fearing that Asante would renege on the proposed charter or turn to the French. In 1874 they had invaded Asante at enormous cost, and to very little profit save for palace loot. Now they invaded again, and duly had their conquest.

Again it proved expensive, but imperial pride was soothed and satisfied. Better still, it was discovered, the expense need not be borne by the British taxpayer. Through a convenient device that would often be repeated, the expense of colonial warfare was transferred to the African taxpayer, who was thus made to pay the cost of his own subjection. The expense in this case was about £450,000 (or about $2,250,000 in the values of 1900). It seems to have taken the finances of the Gold Coast colony, struggling in its early years for the merest solvency, at least two decades to recover from this burden.

And with this imperial factor in full onward rush, plunging ahead like a blinded Cyclops, one may arrive at a rather different assessment of the colonial period. True it is that in many underlying ways, concerned chiefly with the economic trends in play, colonialism in West Africa—or at least in the British colonies of West Africa—can certainly be seen as "episodical." It confirmed those trends. But it did so within an entirely new structure of limits and possibilities. It encouraged production for export, and, in a large sense indeed, this encouragement became the centerpiece of all colonial policy—the great action of what the French aptly called the *mise en valeur* of the new possessions, the "realizing" of their "value." Yet it did this within a framework which, increasingly and systematically, made certain that the lion's share of the "value" thus "realized" should be transferred out of Africa. The imperial factor was preached in the name of the sacred writ of capitalism, or of promoting what was more politely called "free enterprise." But the consequences proved that this imperialism must strike the death knell of any capitalism in Africa that was more than a merely subordinate and fragmentary component of the imperial system itself. In all such ways the colonial epoch was very much more than episodical.

There are other angles of approach that return the same answer. Earlier forms of "profit transfer," such as the slave trade and then the "legitimate" non-slave trade of most of the nineteenth century, had at least left the Africans with a large field of choice. They could build on their own history. They could develop in this way or that. But the colonial period put an end to this relative freedom of choice.

It was not simply that the Africans lost control over their own affairs at all the points that could be decisive—found themselves, as it were, removed from their own history and helplessly implanted in the history of conquerors who proceeded, logically enough from their point of view, to assume that Africans had no history. Far more than that, Africans were placed in a posture of subordination from which they would be able to escape only by taking over the assumptions of their conquerors. The greatest of these assumptions has been that peoples do not exist unless they are nations: further, that they cannot be nations other than on the European model; that is, nations ruled by a bourgeoisie, a "middle class," adhering to the values of the capitalist ethos. *Hinc illae lacrimae*—and all the tears that have flowed from this, as the "parliamentary models" of the late 1950's and early 1960's have one by one crashed or come otherwise to grief, are there to show the consequences.

In colonial Ghana, at least, these assumptions were long in the making, but again they were highly formative of the independent state that Strand has photographed. Lord Grey had laid down the basic doctrine as early as 1853, when some form of permanent British rule in Ghana had begun to seem unavoidable: "The true policy, I believe, [is that we should] keep constantly in sight the formation of a regular [Ghana] government on the European model. . . ." It was, he added, the goal to be eventually attained.

Decades of British rule might pass, centuries might pass; but in the end the Ghanaians should be "formed" to govern themselves "on the European model."

Meanwhile, awaiting these decades or centuries of "formation," there could be gestures. In 1881 an African was nominated to the governor's council: "unofficial" and therefore only a showpiece, and yet a gesture. In 1894 three municipal councils were established. With missionary education, a handful of Africans with a European intellectual formation began to appear on the scene. In 1916, not by accident in a colony which was making no mean contribution to the British war effort, the number of Africans nominated to the legislative council was increased to six—three of whom were drawn from the ranks of these intellectuals, while the others were chiefs. Vigorous little newspapers sprang up under the editorship of men such as Attoh Ahuma. With verve and a fine display of Victorian prose, they dramatized the evils of the "colonial condition" and sought its alleviation. Literary societies and political clubs built platforms for the voicing of European-educated African opinion.

All this likewise contributed to the "model-ness" of the "model colony." The intellectuals, however brilliantly they might depict their handicaps and woes (and they were often brilliant), were caught in the trap that was so fateful for all the newly emergent intelligentsias of the colonies. They were patriotic men who desired progress. But they equated progress with "civilization," and this civilization, as Attoh Ahuma had said, must come inevitably and uniquely from Europe. Moreover, many of them found that the British doctrine here could allow them positions of relative privilege as lawyers and entrepreneurs of one kind or another, or even as civil servants. A recent Nigerian judgment has condemned them as "collaborators." It may be a harsh judgment: after all, given their assumptions, how in the end could they act—save in collaboration with the power which stood for the European civilization in whose saving virtues for Africa they profoundly believed?

Things changed, no doubt, as time went by: but not in essence. The "old intellectuals" of the early 1900's were duly followed by "new intellectuals" after the First World War and into the 1930's. Some

of these, again, were men of scholarly distinction—perhaps none more so than the late Dr. J. B. Danquah, who was to die in prison under Nkrumah's rule. They were "more radical" than their predecessors, but they too accepted the destiny of the "European model." They argued their case in terms of the right of Africans to progress and independence, but also, in practice, in terms of British law and constitutional doctrine: matters in which they had been very well instructed during the years that many of them passed in London's Inns of Court, where Britain trains her men of law.

And the sequence continued. The "new radicals" of the 1930's, Danquah and his like, were duly followed after the Second World War by newer radicals, among whom the most effective and most memorable was undoubtedly Kwame Nkrumah. Some of these "new men," including Nkrumah, had also imbibed wisdom from sources scarcely tapped before. One of these was the Pan-Africanism of black America and the Caribbean; another was the socialism which flowed or seemed to flow from the October Revolution in Russia. Both became large and lasting influences in post-1945 Africa. Each gave rise to much inspiring eloquence and a series of millennial dreams.

Yet neither had any immediate effect. A new yearning by black America for "identification" in a worldwide black community, with Africa as its heart and center, might be very understandable across the Atlantic. It could have little real echo in an Africa that had never doubted its own identity or identities—and least of all in West Africa, where no white settlement had come to reenact the black American experience. The lessons of the October Revolution might be highly relevant, but they proved very hard to hear; and, even when heard, harder still to apply. Only in the 1970's would they begin to make real headway on the continent, though not in Ghana.

Meanwhile there remained, for the "newer radicals" of the 1940's and after, the dominant influence and manifest destiny of "the European model," as well as the economic trends which it appeared to buttress and confirm for traders, professional men, and even cocoa farmers. Accordingly, what nearly all politically thoughtful people in colonial Ghana wanted by the 1950's was no kind of social revolution, but freedom to build this European model on their own account. And by this point the general political position and perspective of the nineteenth century had entirely changed—for the colonized, but also for the colonizers.

On their side, the British came out of the Second World War in a mood for new initiatives. They had been weakened to the point where the evacuation of their Indian empire could only be delayed, no matter how thunderously a Winston Churchill, perennially fighting the last war or the war before that, might rage against any such "betrayal." They had to accept a junior partnership with a United States that looked to the dismantlement of the European empires for reasons of its own. And then, to do them justice, a large proportion of the British people was anti-imperialist, at least in the dour sense that imperialism had been the work of their ruling class.

I would think that no one who lived through those years of anti-colonial struggle would wish for a moment to suggest that decolonization came about smoothly, or painlessly, much less by any concerted "plan." There was no plan. There was only a quickening realization on both sides that decolonization would somehow happen. Just how it was going to happen, and when, remained open questions. Though convinced of its unavoidability, at least in West Africa, the British rulers did their best to delay it. The French, for their part, fought the trend still harder, and in the end gave way only because the British had done so. The Belgians put their heads into their account books and stopped their ears until they were forced to listen. The dictatorship that ruled Portugal simply assumed that nothing new had occurred since the nineteenth century; more than a decade of African armed struggle would be required to bring them up to date.

All the same, decolonization did happen. And, of all the many lands and peoples south of the Sahara, it happened first in the country that Strand has portrayed in this book. It happened in the "model colony."

SIX THE ACHIEVEMENT OF NKRUMAH

Even within the limits of this brief essay, a few dates may be useful as reminders. In 1951 the British conceded a cautious measure of "internal self-rule" to a nationalist ministry, with Kwame Nkrumah as "leader of government business"—he and his ministers still had no real power to govern—and then as prime minister. In 1954, still under nationalist pressure, the British agreed that Ghana should shortly become independent. This was long before they had expected, much less planned, to agree, and dismay or disgust were evident among their fellow imperialists in French Africa and elsewhere. I know the truth of this last point rather well, because in that year I was traveling in the Belgian Congo and Portuguese Angola, and was obliged to listen to the comments of those who ruled there.

In 1957, after further nationalist pressure, Nkrumah was able to assume office as the prime minister of a sovereign state, the first of its kind south of the Sahara, and duly take the ballroom floor with a princess of the British royal family, as was to become the right and proper custom on such British occasions. All was to be forgiven and forgotten: the British are rather good at this sort of thing, having a neat touch with what they have sometimes liked to call the "aristocratic embrace." If any skeletons rattled in the cupboard, at least its doors were firmly shut; and those who might naughtily draw attention to the rattling were not appreciated. (It happened that I was asked to write the script for a documentary film of that great Independence Day. Over the scene of the black prime minister dancing with the white princess, while a glittering crowd stood all around, I had the words: "In other colonies, men are whipped for doing this."

Though perhaps no more than the truth—in Kenya at that time, not to say South Africa, most of the whites would have found them altogether right and obvious —such words were doubtless in the worst of taste: when shown in London, the film was royally disowned and the comment thought deplorable.)

For three years after 1957 a sort of honeymoon prevailed, with Nkrumah carefully acting as the "good boy." Whatever one may think of the wisdom of this in terms of Ghana, it proved a powerful aid to the decolonization of other colonies. Then Nkrumah moved toward trying to realize some of his Pan-African and socialist ideas; and for all those who had thought they had him in their pockets the image of the "good boy" was displaced by that of something like a black devil. In 1960 Ghana became a republic, with Nkrumah as its first—and only—president. An amiable British governor-general retired from the scene and was displaced, in his turn, by a host of eager European "contractor-financiers" promising every kind of heaven to those who would buy their contracts. Some of the debts they managed to foist on Ghana are still extant.

In 1966 a group of army and police officers for whom the "European model" was still a sacrosanct as well as manifest destiny, for their own country or for any other, overthrew the Nkrumah regime, hounded everyone in any way associated with Nkrumah, and set up a military dictatorship. In 1969 they retired from the scene, a great deal the worse for wear and lamented by very few, in favor of a new parliamentary regime under a professional sociologist turned politician, Dr. Kofi Busia. In 1972 this regime was in turn discarded after another military take-over led by Colonel Ignatius Acheampong. Colonel Acheampong and his colleagues explained that they had acted on the grounds that the parliamentary regime had become authoritarian, incompetent and corrupt, and the great majority seemed to agree, or, at least, said nothing to the contrary.

Ousted from power in 1966 while on a peace mission to the Far East, Nkrumah retired to none of those villas in Switzerland that he was fancifully supposed to possess but in fact did not. He retired to Africa, where he took refuge with his old friend Presi-

dent Sékou Touré of the Republic of Guinea, several hundred miles along the coast from Ghana. There he bid defiance to the military group who had ousted him, and set about recording their misdeeds. He went on writing, and published several more books. On April 27, 1972, at the age of sixty-three, he died in a Rumanian hospital where he was being treated for what was reported to be cancer.

His body was brought back to Conakry, the capital of Guinea, and then, after some negotiation, was sent on to Accra at the request of the new military government that had thrown out Dr. Busia. There it was given the full honors of the state, and buried quietly at Nkrumah's native village in southwestern Ghana. Even his Ghanaian enemies, now that he was dead, found it well to admit that their country had lost the most famous man it had ever known. The new head of state, Acheampong, saw no difficulty in saying so. "Today," he said in his message to Nkrumah's mother, "we mourn the loss of a great leader whose place in history is assured."

But what kind of place? A large and leading one, yes: beyond that, however, no one could be certain. Perhaps because he was the first "colonial black" to speak boldly for an African sovereign state, he raised tremendous controversies during his lifetime. The more conservative of British newspapers wavered between condemning him as a tyrant or a mountebank. Those who sympathized, or wished to sympathize, varied between warm admiration and embarrassed astonishment. Foreign businessmen praised him when they got contracts, or, when they did not, came away with bitter scorn. Others, more on the left of opinion, swallowed far more propaganda than was good for them, only to spew it out later on with angry accusations of betrayal. A wide variety of Marxist thinkers tried to come to terms with what he was doing or saying, but they too found this difficult. No serious observer knew quite what to think of him.

There was corresponding controversy in Ghana itself, made all the livelier by the good old Ghana custom of kicking hard and kicking often. There were, of course, many who were proud of him and of what he had done or was trying to do; and these included a large number of otherwise humble people. There were others, ambitious or simply greedy, who got together a claque of deafening adulation that was supposed to conceal, but seldom did, the rattle of the government money that was going into their private pockets. Yet others understood both his policy and his predicament, and worked with an heroic self-effacement to advance the one and ease the other.

But then there was the Ghana opposition. For them, and notably for their intellectual spokesmen, there was really nothing too bad that one could say about Nkrumah. Monstrous, vain and dictatorial, oppressive, dishonest and insincere, corrupt and plain silly: the Ghana opposition began saying such things almost as soon as Nkrumah had won "internal self-rule" in 1951, and they went on saying them, with a venom and vigor that never faltered, right until the end. They said them while Nkrumah was trying to work the "European model," and they said them after he had given up that fairly hopeless exercise. Plots were mounted against him, bombs were thrown, shots were fired, all aiming at his life; and in each such plot Ghanaian individuals led the way.

Now that he is gone it is a little easier to think calmly about this always remarkable and emotive man. One is allowed, for example, to think of him as one knew him (and I knew him myself, though never intimately, from 1952 until 1965): as a man of constant interest in his friends and fellow workers, and of a constant kindness to them whenever kindness could help; or as a thinker with an endless curiosity and love of knowledge, always collecting books, perpetually reading; or, in another dimension, as a tribune whose feelings and beliefs, as befits a tribune, came out more strongly than the thought that supported them; or again, and perhaps above all, as a partner in conversation whose limits lay wherever logic or originality could push them.

It may still be too early to form any useful opinion about the value of his intellectual and political gifts. During his time in office they were often obscured by the sheer problems of making headway against a host of troubles. They were also obscured by the consequences of his vanity, and he developed a gross amount of vanity. The principles of social change for which he stood with increasing clarity dur-

ing the 1960's were similarly muddled or frustrated by the habits of opportunism he had cultivated—had needed to cultivate—during the 1950's. He looked far ahead, but failed to inspect the ground beneath his feet. Yet the central fact remains: Nkrumah was a man who made great things happen. Three great things.

The first was that he led to independence the first black colony to win free of colonial rule and in so doing opened the way for others and smoothed their path. The second was that he gave this newly independent country an organic unity, and a sense of unity within itself, that it had not possessed before. The third was that he went beyond these achievements. He saw and said that the "European model" simply could not work to Africa's advantage. However confusedly, he came entirely to reject the mechanistic or reductive view which held (and often holds) that Africa's position can be no more than a "periphery" of the world's "developed center."

Along that line of thought he stood foursquare for an eventual unification of African countries within a framework which could realize Africa's potentials, over and beyond the narrow limits possible to forty or so feeble nation-states. He came nowhere near realizing these aims of socialism and union. He made several large blunders or miscalculations in working for them. But who, in this context, is going to throw the first stone? A great part of his merit, one may think, will be seen in the fact that he proclaimed these aims, and proclaimed them at a time when the saving vision they projected was of a profound psychological value to countless people outside his own country, or even outside his own continent. This third achievement, no doubt, is what accounts for the penetrating resonance that his name retains today.

Of these three things, though, it is probably the first that will be thought to have counted for most. One of modern Africa's outstanding political thinkers, Amilcar Cabral, said in 1972 that Nkrumah was "the strategist of genius in the struggle against classical colonialism"; and Cabral was a man who measured his words. So it may be right to complete this essay with a bird's-eye view of what that struggle meant, and of how it was conducted.

SEVEN "LEAD KINDLY LIGHT..."

Many have described the scene of action and the "truths" that governed it. Not surprisingly, few agree. Was the colonial mission a good thing or was it the reverse? Does it deserve its claim to have advanced Africans to the threshold of the modern world, handed them the keys to entry, and then magnanimously withdrawn—only to find, as many liked to prophesy must happen, that the Africans would stumble across that threshold and fall upon their faces?

Some have said no. Others have dissented. Yet even these others have often found it possible, during the 1970's, to say that those "first independences" in which Ghana led the way were a sham and a delusion, or barely worth the trouble. And this, of course, is only another way of saying that there was some other policy for shaking off colonial rule, and that Africans should have found it.

My own view is that all such opinions are false to the realities of Africa in the wake of the Second World War. One did not in fact imagine, in those years of anti-colonial agitation, that the triumphant end of the exercise should be a series of independences that would celebrate the victory of the "European model." What one thought—or at least what I thought (and was very far from being alone in my thinking)—was that independence on the European model was a necessary step, because it was unavoidable, but that it could never be more than a transitional step of ambiguous value. Those who thought otherwise were to be correspondingly "disillusioned," whether with Nkrumah or Nkrumah's Ghana or other such personalities and emergences; but the disillusionment rested on a lack of realism in respect to the possible options available.

Looking back, it may be agreed, as we have seen, that the colonial period "worked out" many of the themes dominant in pre-colonial Ghana, or, more widely, in pre-colonial Africa: the continued growth of the existing economy, but also its continued distortion in favor of foreign beneficiaries; the partnership with foreign capital always desired by the coastal traders, and eventually accepted even by the rulers of Asante; the unfolding, though in new and more exasperated ways, of the country's regional rivalries. All these were parts of the process of foreign rule that found many local partners. In all these respects a termination in the European model, or in what its critics have preferred to call "neo-colonialism," became altogether likely.

The real question, of course, was always what could or should follow that "termination"; and in this respect the Ghana that Nkrumah led presents a case of quite extraordinary interest. Yet the question could not even be posed, much less answered, before the people of Ghana became free to consider it. And it is in this aspect, above all, that the colonial experience was almost entirely negative. For it was above all a period of cultural suffocation and psychological discouragement, of barriers to useful knowledge, to self-respect, to any understanding of the dynamics of the modern world, and of Africa's possible connection with those dynamics.

West Africa suffered less than other colonial regions. British rule here was generally benevolent, or at least tolerantly paternal. But it still remained a racist rule that supposed the absolute superiority of Europeans and the manifest inferiority of Africans. When early nationalists such as Casely Hayford raised their voices against the systematic discrimination, contempt or indifference from which they said they suffered, they were not imagining these handicaps. They really suffered them. This was true in a large and general sense: in the calculated suppression of all "unorthodox" ideas, in the persecution of intellectual rebels, in the clapping of capacious blinkers on the minds of all those who could manage to get to school. It was true in a merely material sense. There might be thirty-six hospitals for four or five million Africans in 1936; there were also seven hospitals for 3,000 Europeans. And what went for the hospitals went for every other aspect of public life. Even if they try, those who did not experience colonial Africa may still find it hard to imagine the narrowness and pettiness and general misery of "colonial ideas," or the situation in which these "ideas" existed and persisted.

The designated leaders of African opinion, the educated elite, were possibly in still worse condition. Like the French, the British firmly believed in the value of educating and promoting a privileged group of Africans who might eventually become their partners in the grand imperial enterprise. Nothing shows this better than the loyalties that these Africans developed, and that they would duly translate into universities which aped the great examples of Oxford or the Sorbonne. These African universities might have been expected to become the powerhouses of new ideas, new programs, new policies, new methods of development. As it was, they became universities peopled by distinguished men and women who hankered for a lost and even legendary past. To borrow a phrase, they became part of the problem: the problem of generating an indigenous development rather than a mere growth of the "inherited situation."

Even that growth was hard to see during the colonial period. Nkrumah afterwards summed up a balance sheet of what had been done or not done in Ghana: a partial balance, if you like, and yet one that tells a good deal about the scene of action. Always more interested in the future than in the past, he wrote one of the few passages of his published writings concerned with the colonial record of his own country. He recalled the time when he and his colleagues, Kojo Botsio, Komlo Gbedemah and others, first took office in 1951 and were able to inspect administrative realities for the first time "from the inside." They could then measure, to some extent, the real gains of colonial rule against the real losses. And what they found was of little comfort to those who preferred to think of the colonial episode as a constructive effort of the rich to help the poor, or of the strong to aid the weak.

"The housing situation when we took office," he wrote, "was shocking. It reflected what appeared to be a standard European view of the African attitude towards domestic shelter: anything that keeps off the rain and offers shade from the sun is good enough. . . . In all the years that the British colonial office administered this country, hardly any serious rural water development was carried out. What this means is not easy to convey to readers who take for granted that they have only to turn on a tap to get an immediate supply of good drinking water. This, if it had occurred to our rural communities, would have been their idea of heaven. They would have been grateful for a single village well or stand-pipe.

"As it was, after a hard day's work in the hot and humid fields, men and women would return to their village and then have to tramp for as long as two hours with a pail or pot in which, at the end of their outward journey, they would be lucky to collect some brackish germ-filled water from what may perhaps have been little more than a swamp. Then there was the long journey back. Four hours a day for an inadequate supply of water for washing and drinking, water for the most part disease-ridden! This picture was true for almost the whole country. . . ."

Why was it true? Nkrumah went on to point out that water development, like other such things, was costly. Being no more than a basic public service, there could be no profit in it. It gave no immediate prospect of economic return. And then colonial government was always "poor": not, indeed, because the colonies in question were necessarily poor, but because all the revenues must come from colonial taxpayers who were, for the most part, "underdeveloped peasants." The "mother country" might rejoice in the comfortable thought of doing good, but she was certainly not going to pay the cost of it. No money—therefore no development of supplies of water.

Perhaps: but Nkrumah, like others, was not fooled by the argument. "A fraction of the profits being taken out of the country by the business and mining interests," he replied, "would have covered the cost of a first-class water system." This was scarcely an exaggeration. If the Gold Coast was poor in local tax-yielding capacity, it was very far from poor in other senses that were more important. Foreign trading companies and mining enterprises made a great deal of money. But they, of course, were not taxed, or were taxed only in the most nominal way. Here lay another principle of colonial rule—a principle that was rigidly observed. Consider, for example, the record of mining profits and taxation.

In 1952 there came into my hands an official Gold Coast government document marked *Confidential: Limited Circulation*. This was a "Memorandum on Mining in the Gold Coast" which did much credit to the British official who wrote it. Reading this thoughtful document, one easily discovered why it was to be kept out of circulation. It argued a most powerful case against the government's taxation policy, and it exposed just how much the local European-owned mining companies had long been getting away with, and were still getting away with. It said that "the government's record of social and general development in the mining areas is open to adverse criticism," and it pleaded for the retention in the country of a larger share of exported profits. It showed that as much as *half* of the total proceeds of mining for gold, diamonds and manganese were transferred annually out of the Gold Coast, whereas what remained was mostly eaten up by payments for the import of machinery and other goods, and by relatively high salaries for European staffs. The latter received in 1949, for example, no less than £830,000 for a total return of £6.4 million. Alongside this, taxation was insignificant. "In spite of exports amounting to as high as £5,583,905 in a single year," an American historian of the Gold Coast had commented a few years earlier, "the [gold] mines remained until 1944 with no levy on their exports other than insignificant rents to the chiefs and a slight tax of the government. All income tax was paid in England itself."

This is where a major evil of the colonial period is revealed. Wealth there was in Ghana, even considerable wealth, but it was not a source that Ghana could draw upon. I do not know how much of this wealth was shipped abroad in taxless profits; perhaps no one will ever know. It was certainly much. "During the last thirty years of British colonial administration," Ghanaian sources have estimated for their part, "British trading and shipping interests took out of the country a total of £300 millions." This, then, is the background against which one must review all claims to the effect that "because the African colonies were poor, little could be done for them." This is where one may see that the colonial period did much

more than merely "work out" preexisting trends, but greatly influenced these trends to the greater disadvantage of the peoples who labored to produce the profits.

Not even colonial barriers to understanding could quite obscure such truths. Colonial Ghana knew several large movements of protest, notably by cocoa farmers objecting to the prices they were paid. These protests duly flowed into the anti-colonial movement of a new nationalism which arose in the wake of the Second World War. Then the politics of minority protest—of polite intellectual pressure for the "European model," moderate, gradualist, content with small gains—was swept away by the politics of mass upheaval.

Many influences combined to make this happen. One of them was the growing number of elementary school graduates who came from an expansion of such schools, a numerical expansion in which the British could take some pride. These were the "verandah boys," as the educated elite contemptuously called them; and they were not content to wait for any slow unfolding of a European model in the course of God's good time and British policy. Another influence was the return home of volunteers who had fought against Nazi Germany, Fascist Italy, imperialist Japan. These were many. By the end of 1945 no fewer than 63,038 Ghanaians were serving in the British Army, and 41,880 of these were serving outside their own country. As many as 30,500 went through the fearful rigors of the Burma campaign; others were battle troops on the East African fronts that saw the end of Fascist Italian rule in Ethiopia.

By the time these soldiers came home, they had seen much and learned much. Returning to a second-class citizenship, they were asked to become once more the docile objects of colonial rule. It had happened before. Back in 1914, at the beginning of the First World War, the Gold Coast had likewise given generously to the British cause. When that war was over, the *Gold Coast Independent* had commented in some well-remembered words that if African volunteers "were good enough to fight and die in the Empire's cause, they were good enough to have a share in the government of their countries." The volunteers of the Second World War had the same thought, but they had it with a new vehemence and conviction. The times were ripe for change.

Yet the position at the end of 1947, when Nkrumah and his friend Kojo Botsio stepped off the boats that had brought them from England, was seemingly placid. On the surface, at any rate, all appeared calm, and, to outward seeming, the Gold Coast was still a model colony embalmed in colonial routine. Its established politicians might be critical of government, but at best they were a very small group who spoke for chiefs and professional men, and whose naturally conservative approaches and connections were averse to any radical change. No radical change seemed in prospect, much less any thought of revolution.

Nkrumah had been long abroad—ten years in the United States and another two in England—and he needed time to find his feet again. He went home to see his mother and then, with reservations, took up his work as general secretary of the new nationalist party, the United Gold Coast Convention, lately formed by Danquah and others of the parliamentary elite. He was in for an exciting time, though it scarcely appeared so at the start.

The British thought they had the situation well in hand, and there were reasons for such thinking. Government revenue and expenditure had more than doubled over the years after the First World War, and this, even when allowing for depreciation in the value of sterling, showed a modest improvement on what had gone before. Cocoa exports had likewise more than doubled in monetary value; more significantly, the share of cocoa in Ghana's total export trade had fallen from about 74 percent in 1921 to about 46 percent in 1946, revealing an expansion in the kind of goods that Ghana could produce. Railway mileage had similarly doubled, from 276 miles of track in 1921 to 536 in 1947; the mileage of motorable roads had increased from 2,241 to 8,114, of which 620 were sprayed with tar. An even more convincing sign of technological change was the vast increase in the number of motor vehicles in use: in 1921 there had been only 470; no count was made, it seems, in 1946–47, but by 1959–60 the total would swell to just under 50,000.

There had also been some progress on the side of political change. Governor Sir Alan Burns had decided, even before the war was over, that Gold Coast Africans must at last be given a larger share in seeing how decisions were made, and even to some extent in helping to make decisions. His new constitution of 1946 accordingly widened the membership of the legislative council to include no fewer than eighteen Africans out of a total of thirty-two. Crucial matters of policy and action remained in the Governor's hands, and, as a British political scientist, Martin Wight, observed at the time, "the change in democracy [was] only at the top and not at the bottom." Even so, another British political scientist, Dennis Austin, may be right in claiming that this constitution "brought the country as a whole to the clearly defined stage of representative government," or, more accurately, to the point where that stage could begin. In any case, the Governor thought that he was well abreast of the development of "native opinion." Congratulations were duly exchanged at the official level: again in Wight's contemporary words, "the Colonial Office and the Governor no doubt hope that the constitution will for several decades satisfy the legitimate aspirations of the political class."

At this point, however, the political class, the established elite, was not satisfied. They believed—and events would prove them right—that a local reincarnation of the British parliamentary model was now advanced to the point where Africans could take charge of it. They were all the more of this opinion from being highly aware that popular and possibly turbulent currents of opinion were also on the scene; and they concluded, again rightly, that these currents might outrun their own position of leadership and engulf them. Before 1947 was out, accordingly, their best and leading spokesman, who was Danquah, took the lead in forming the United Gold Coast Convention, a party pledged "to ensure that by all legitimate and constitutional means the control and direction of the Government shall within the shortest time possible pass into the hands of the people and their Chiefs." The British were not displeased. "All legitimate and constitutional means" exercised in "the shortest time possible" could not seem very worrying, at least for the foreseeable future.

But underlying pressures now surfaced. On February 28, 1948, Accra was suddenly the scene of "disturbances" which took a violent form. These spread. By March 16, when they were brought to an end, the military had been called in to help the police. Twenty-nine people had been killed and over two hundred were being treated for wounds; the country lay under a "state of emergency"; and a new governor, Sir Gerald Creasy, quietly informed the new legislative council that he had been "overtaken by events." The political class could only sympathize: their own case was no better.

Their aim, after all, was to shoehorn "the people" into a parliamentary model which they should control. As later events would abundantly illustrate, their preferred method was to use popular pressure—up to a point: the point beyond which it could become dangerous to their own claims. Their underlying interests were therefore closer to those of the British than to those of "the people." Each had a comparable concern with the maintenance of a "law and order" in which "the people"—the unwashed masses, the "verandah boys," the ex-servicemen, and any possible competitors among the trading community— would stay strictly in their place.

This was clear from the organization of their party when Nkrumah arrived, at Danquah's invitation, to act as its secretary. "When I took up my appointment," he was to recall in his autobiography of 1957, "I found, on going through the minute book, that thirteen branches had been formed throughout the country. On looking further into the matter, however, I discovered that this was entirely incorrect. In actual fact, just a couple of branches had been established and these were inactive." In the minds of its founders, the new party was to be a painted back-cloth for a parliamentary pressure group. But in Nkrumah's mind the new party would have to become much more than that if it were to prove of any value.

"I saw at once the urgent need for a country-wide tour with the object of setting up branches of the UGCC in every part of the country. The results of

this were most successful, for within six months I had established 500 branches in the Colony alone [in the coastal areas, that is, to the south of Asante]. I issued membership cards, collected dues, and started by raising funds in one way and another for the organisation so that in a short while I was able to open a banking account on behalf of the Working Committee."

In this way the elementary school graduates, the "commoners," the despised "verandah boys" and many other humble folk found their way into practical politics, and took a hand in shaping the future. Understandably, from their point of view, the colonial authorities were disturbed. They lost little time in arresting Nkrumah and his principal associates. Even before this was accomplished, however, Nkrumah was already the target of some sharp criticism from his employers of the educated elite. The din of those marching feet, the shouts of those triumphant demonstrations addressed by Nkrumah and his aides, the talk in those multiplying branches: all this was not a music they could welcome.

Duly released from political imprisonment, Nkrumah at once found himself under heavy attack from Dr. Danquah and others, and soon, he recalls, "it became obvious that they were determined to rid themselves of me, at all costs." The police who arrested him had rifled his belongings and found among them an unsigned membership card of the British Communist Party. Nkrumah himself denied then and later that this had any significance other than that while in England he had associated himself "with all parties from the extreme right to the extreme left in order to gain as much knowledge as I could." Though he had leanings toward Marxism, as some of his writings and actions confirmed, he had never joined any foreign party.

The police, of course, came to their own conclusions. So did the established leaders of the United Gold Coast Convention. "In due course I was faced with various charges by the Working Committee. As I expected, they were fearfully excited about the word 'Comrade.' To them the word was obviously synonymous with Communism! 'Is this not proof that he is a Communist?' they asked."

On that ground, as it happened, most of the

members of the British Labour Party, who not only called each other "comrade" but even liked to sing "The Red Flag" on ceremonial occasions, would have been revealed as agents of Moscow. It is even possible that Dr. Danquah and his colleagues believed they were. But whatever Danquah and his friends really thought on this point, they had had enough of their general secretary. They found him a nuisance; they also found him dangerous. They asked him to resign, and offered him a one-way ticket back to England.

They reckoned without their man. Nkrumah responded by calling a mass meeting at Saltpond, not far down the coast from Accra, on June 12, 1949, and there declared the formation of a new party, a party of the masses. To the UGCC slogan of "self-government within the shortest possible time" he now opposed the slogan "self-government NOW." And to the tune of a venerable missionary hymn, "Lead Kindly Light," the Convention People's Party was born. Within a year the CPP had overturned the whole colonial situation in the Gold Coast. By 1950 the constitution of 1946, framed to last for "several decades," lay in ruins. Arrested again in 1950, Nkrumah and his principal colleagues were brought out of prison in 1951, in the wake of a general election which had given Nkrumah's party as many as thirty-four seats in the reformed colonial legislature. Catching up with themselves, the British gave way at once, and "internal self-rule" followed as the prelude to an eventual independence. The politics of mass protest had won their first victory.

It was a very limited victory, even so, and the leaders of Nkrumah's CPP were aware of this. They still had no real power, most of which remained in the hands of the governor. Further progress would have to mean a full acceptance of the British model with all its implications. There was no question that they might refuse it. If they had, the men of the UGCC would have jumped at the chance of doing what the CPP rejected, and public opinion would have backed them in doing so, for public opinion would not have understood rejection. Aside from that, there was only a handful of CPP leaders who would have gone along with rejection, and they were men of no great stand-

ing in the political scene. To most of the leaders of the CPP, and to all or nearly all of its "old guard," rejection would have been an act of folly.

Nkrumah reaped the fruits of this "tactical action," as he called it (or "tactful action," as some preferred), and proceeded to become the "good boy" whom the British should be taught to rely upon and trust.

Six years were to pass before "internal self-rule" became sovereignty. They were extremely difficult years. Seeing themselves outdistanced, the leaders of the opposition set themselves to wage a bitter battle against any further British concessions to the man whom they now cordially hated, and to the party they as cordially despised. Moreover, in large fields of policy there could be no change, since the government had no power to make any. What the government had to do, through the CPP, was to unify the country behind a program demanding independence. It was a large task, and it took up most of the party's energies.

Two regional challenges met the CPP almost at once. The first came from the northern territories, beyond Asante, whose peoples belonged to historical cultures and traditions different from those of the forest or the coastland. Their chiefs, moreover, distrusted the CPP because they tended to fear domination by the more numerous populations of the south. They organized the Northern People's Party for the 1954 elections, and managed to win twelve out of the twenty-one seats then available to the Northern Territories.

A more important challenge was to follow in Asante. This took the initial form of a new opposition party called the National Liberation Movement. To some extent the NLM was a successor to the now defunct UGCC of the educated elite. To some extent it was also an instrument of the traditional chiefs and traditional powers of Asante, organized in the Asanteman council under the chairmanship of the greatest chief of all, the king of Asante himself. As pressure for independence grew stronger and wider, these chiefs of the forestland became more apprehensive. They believed, not without reason, that independence under the CPP might well be fatal to their power; and in this respect, of course, their thinking was no different from that of many other chiefs in colonial Africa. Time after time they sent delegations to London, usually headed by the sociologist Dr. Kofi Busia, who pleaded with the British government and public to set their face against granting independence to a country under CPP rule. Though sympathetically received by conservative British newspapers, these delegations failed to persuade the imperial government of their case, just as they failed at home outside the areas of their electoral strength. When their campaign against independence came to nothing, violence began to take a hand. CPP premises in Asante were stormed and wrecked, many CPP supporters were driven out, and, with the inevitable reply-in-kind by local members of the CPP, casualties rapidly multiplied. On November 10, 1955, there was even an attempt to blow up Nkrumah's house on an evening when Nkrumah was holding a conference there.

Through all this, Nkrumah remained faithful to his belief in mass organization and agitation. His maxim might well have been that of a famous black American, Frederick Douglass, who declared in 1857 that in matters of this kind "if there is no struggle, there is no progress. Those who prefer to favour freedom, and yet deprecate agitation, are men who want crops without ploughing up the ground. They want the ocean without the awful roar of its many waters." Following this line of thought, the CPP made gains. It still failed to carry the majority of potential voters, but it carried the great majority of those who actively desired that their country should move forward to a different future. It had all the ideas that were new and hopeful. It possessed a clear monopoly of political dynamism. In 1954 Nkrumah and his colleagues felt strong enough to lay before the British a formal demand for immediate independence.

The British were ready to listen. It would now have been extremely difficult and costly to have attempted to turn the tide or even to dam it up for long. Also, it was the general British colonial policy to "pick the winner" before colonial independence, in the hope that the winner would then become a convenient junior partner. A third and lesser reason lay in the excellent personal relations between Nkrumah and the then governor, Sir Charles Arden-Clarke.

Yet the British were also hesitant. They wanted a slower rate of change, and one they could control. Their condition of acceptance was that the Gold Coast should hold another general election: if this produced a result that was clearly favorable for the party which stood for independence, then independence would follow without delay. Nkrumah tried to refuse this condition. He argued that little had changed since the CPP's clear majority of 1954: why hold another election two years later? Besides, he feared that an electoral campaign might further envenom the bitterness in Asante. London remained adamant, however, and another election was duly held. This again brought the CPP a clear parliamentary majority. Given the British commitment, there could now be no further argument. It remained only to fix the crucial date.

This was to be March 6, 1957.

Nkrumah has told the story in the very diplomatic words of his autobiography of 1957. "It was Monday, September 17th. I had a full morning's work ahead of me and I was going over my diary of appointments." He knew that the date was on the way from London, but London had delayed in fixing it. "Suddenly there was a ring from the telephone that connected me with the Governor.

" 'Good morning, P.M. [Prime Minister],' said Sir Charles. 'I just wanted to tell you that I had received some good news for you. I wondered if you could come up and see me for a few minutes when you are free.'

" 'Yes, certainly, Sir Charles,' I said, as I hurriedly scanned through my appointments. 'I'm afraid this morning is pretty hectic—would three o'clock this afternoon be all right?'

"I arrived at Government House promptly. If there had been any doubts in my mind as to the contents of the message awaiting me, the look of pleasure on Sir Charles's face as I entered his office swept it away at once. He shook me firmly and warmly by the hand and then handed me a despatch from the Secretary of State, Mr. Alan Lennox-Boyd, then in charge of the British Colonial Office. There were . . . a number of long paragraphs. When I reached the fifth one, however, the tears of joy that I had difficulty hiding blurred the rest of the document.

"After a few minutes I raised my eyes to meet those of the Governor. For some moments there was nothing either of us could say. Perhaps we were both looking back over the seven years of our association, beginning with doubts, growth of trust, sincerity and friendship, and now, finally, this moment of victory for us both, a moment beyond description and a moment that could never be entirely recaptured."

I have given this long quotation because it illustrates so very well the ambiguities of the situation. Six years of "tactful action" had produced the desired result. But had they not produced something else as well? Wasn't there the possibility that this emotional meeting between two "old friends and colleagues," the nationalist leader and the colonial governor, stood for rather more than might appear? There were some, though they were very few, who soon said so. They saw the result as very nearly a sellout to all those forces in the nationalist movement, whether commercial or bureaucratic or merely eager for a profitable place in the sun, who would be quite content with the spoils of office, and who, indeed, really wanted nothing else.

Such trends had greatly strengthened since 1951. They were entirely dominant in 1957, so that there was still less of a chance that the CPP would take any kind of radical course than in 1951. Great issues of choice had no interest for most of its dominant members. All through those years, they had calmly accepted the policies proposed by the British or by similarly conservative advisers, all of whom had combined to explain that any wicked action designed to make the economy less dependent on the world market must be disastrous, for it would "frighten off" all those foreign investors whose good will was said to be essential to any progress. This had led to a steady refusal to improve the price paid to cocoa producers; and this in turn had inflamed among cocoa producers a well-justified sense of gross injustice. The CPP would pay a sore political price for this.

To some extent, the CPP was still a widely popular party: people wanted independence, after all, and the CPP held the purse strings of a lot of useful patronage. But the popularity was much eroded. It would become more so. Meanwhile, the immediate gains were not small, and they were thoroughly enjoyed in a country which likes to enjoy itself.

The ceremonies on that fine March day of independence were nothing if not impressive. Descending on Ghana for the first time in history, an army of pressmen from all over the world had a foretaste of the love of display and largeness of gesture which were to mark the new regime, and which, later on, were to be added to the list of its crimes by those whom Nkrumah would enrage or disappoint. Important people came from important countries. One of them was Richard Nixon in his vice-presidential dignity. It happened to me, as I remember, that I walked behind Nixon across the tarmac of Accra airport. Halfway over, he spotted a crowd of spectators waving flags, and made a sharp turn toward them, saying to his surprised Ghanaian host, "Let's go and shake hands with the voters." It was that sort of occasion.

There were agreeable festivities. The king of Asante had refused to come from Kumase, but lesser chiefs came. A durbar gathered them in their golden robes and panoplies amidst the splendor of twirling umbrellas and the beat of drums. I remember coming across Dr. Danquah attired in leopard skin and ceremonial equipment in the suite of a famous Akan chief. Though Danquah was one of Nkrumah's most bitter opponents, he was also a man with a vivid sense of history. Even he was happy on that day.

Others felt otherwise. A day or two earlier, that same famous chief of the Akan had received me in the throne room of his house in the forest country. His mood was one of sadness. He could see no good in what had now occurred. The gentlemen would be thrust aside; the mob would take over, and God alone knew what the mob might do. "Ah, my boy," he said, shaking his handsome head, "it all began with that man Creech-Jones [former Colonial Secretary in Britain's post-war Labour government and a determined if cautious supporter of African independence]. Now we have a gentleman in charge, Mr. Lennox Boyd [Colonial Secretary in the then Conservative British government]. He will try to do the right thing. But it is too late, too late."

Up in Kumase, center of the traditionalist opposition to the CPP, members of the elite had been even more emphatic, and had spoken openly of the possibility that they would have to revolt. As events were soon to show; some of those who talked like this meant what they said. Yet not for another eleven years would their hopes be realized.

The new rulers now began to look into financial and other such confidential files that they had not been able to see before, and to take stock of the position. In one respect, at least, it was wonderfully good. There was plenty of cash in the national till. Thanks to diligent milking of the cocoa farmers, by means of government-controlled purchasing arrangements which kept the price paid to producers far below the world price, the regime inherited sterling assets of around £200 million. The new government proceeded to secure control of these assets, and then to spend them. The prudence of their spending is arguable. But the real point is that the existence of these relatively very large assets meant that the "inherited situation," at least for the time being, was thoroughly viable. Very poor countries, such as Tanzania or Guinea-Bissau, might afterwards begin their independent lives with nothing or almost nothing in the till. They were accordingly faced with an unavoidable need to confront the sources of poverty, and to look for policies that were very different from those of the European model. Not so Ghana.

A large part of these initial assets were spent in the years that followed. Most of the outlay went into useful and even necessary infrastructure. Much went into education and health services. Some went into large industrial projects of a more doubtful immediate value, such as the great Akosombo Dam on the Volta River, a deep-water port at Teme, and an oil refinery. A small part went into Nkrumah's plans to help other nationalist parties with money—and he helped many —and into forwarding his schemes for union by organizing large conferences of nationalist parties from all over Africa; and this part paid large political dividends for the cause of African independence in those years. Another small part went into prestige buildings and useless pomp. And a still smaller part, yet a crudely blatant one, went into private pockets.

Ghana became, in any case, a far more agreeable and comfortable country than it had ever been before. Society expanded, came alive, acquired a new self-confidence, tapped the springs of many kinds of cultural talent. Books by Ghanaian writers began to appear, and also to be published in Ghana. Films were made, plays were written and performed, poets found their voices. Popular music flourished; so did the arts of drum and dancing. The tone of all this was exciting, controversial, argumentative: the tone of people who begin talking to each other after a long silence. There was much radio in many local languages, and eventually TV with a promising educational content.

The constrictions of the colonial period receded. Between 1951 and 1961, for example, the number of children at primary school increased from about 211,000 to about 484,000, and the comparable expansion in post-primary schools was of the same order. Primary school fees had been abolished in 1952; nine years later, primary schooling was made compulsory. In 1951 the Gold Coast had turned out six university graduates; in 1961 the number was 148, with a further large expansion on the way.

Ghanaian critics were to say that educational standards had been drastically lowered, and to some extent they were right. Standards undoubtedly were lowered from the narrowly selective elitism of the secondary-schooling system of the colonial period, when the critics had received their own education. That must always happen during a rapid educational expansion from a slender starting base. Indeed, standards probably were lowered more than was reasonably avoidable. But to the anti-Nkrumah critics *any* lowering of standards must be tantamount to crime, because it would always tend to devalue and lead to an entrenchment upon the higher-educational monopoly of the few. These critics, one may confidently add, did not include the parents of all those children now getting to secondary school who could never have gotten there before.

There were other reforms and improvements to the end of Ghana's becoming more comfortable and capable of responding to its people's ideas about progress. Still, much poverty remained. Average living standards were barely improved; in some sectors they were tending even to fall. All this the reader will glimpse in some of Strand's most moving photographs, for none of the basic factors of impoverishment present in an economy still essentially colonial had yet been tackled. These were the factors of impoverishment whose influence would soon thrust their way to the front.

Yet these were not factors of spiritual or cultural impoverishment. In everything that "spiritual and cultural" may be taken to mean, those years have left a vivid memory of enrichment and release. The "atmosphere" of the 1950's, when Ghanaians first began to feel that they were about to repossess their own country, or when they began to take over departments in the government and other responsibilities hitherto barred to them, or discuss an entirely different future in their newspapers and meetings, or merely enjoy everyday freedoms they had not had before: all this was far from the frustrations and the boredom of colonial times; and the contrast was greatly to the advantage of the country that Nkrumah led.

EIGHT THE 1960's AND AFTER

Someone, it may have been myself, has called "honeymoon years" the first and earliest period of Ghana's independence: the years up to 1960 or possibly 1961. And the description, even if it was mine, is not a bad one.* Married to independence under the most respectable of auspices and after a very long betrothal, launched upon domestic bliss by ceremonies of the most orthodox liturgy and consecration, with a British conservative government as best man and the British royal family in attendance, Ghana seemed to have everything going for it—at least to those who liked that kind of thing.

Free enterprise was all the rage, and not yet, as it afterwards became, all the outrage too. Capitalism was definitely in. Wayward thoughts about any other system were as definitely out. Representing the first black state to emerge from colonial toils (Guinea, the next one, would have to wait another eighteen months), Nkrumah paid calls abroad, brought a fresh but tactful contribution to the councils of the great, made his mark as a member of the British Commonwealth conference of prime ministers, and skillfully epitomized the African presence wherever the world discussed its business. As Dr. A. L. Adu, one of this Ghana's eminent civil servants, would say much later, Nkrumah made "Africans everywhere feel proud of their Africanness."

In all these ways, tactfully or not, this Ghana put the world to school about the reality of Africa and its civilizations, about the humanity of black folk, about the truths of their present as well as their past. But after 1960, or more exactly after 1961, the honeymoon with respectability came rather quickly to an end. The grittier aspects of domestic bliss insisted on their presence, and ever more rudely. Times changed; men and women with them. Inside Africa, the "first independences"—very many by 1963—began to lose their shine. Outside Africa, there came romantic disillusionment: these independent Africans, apparently, were not going to be the angels of wisdom and light they were supposed to have become in the moment of their emergence from colonial darkness. As early as 1962, when much of Africa was still under colonial rule, a Frenchman published a book entitled *Black Africa Has Made a Bad Start*. The title, if not the book, became widely quoted. Another kind of start, it was implied, should have been made; and the Africans, it was implied, should obviously have chosen it.

Nkrumah continued to rule until 1966, when the soldiers moved against him. That was also the year when other soldiers moved against the first federation of Nigeria. Soon, all sorts of military ambitions filled the African picture. Perhaps 1966 really

* Readers who wish for a detailed account may care to refer to my *Black Star: A View of the Life and Times of Kwame Nkrumah*, Longman, London, and Praeger, New York, 1973.

marks, at least in most of West Africa, the end of the "first independences" and the beginning of new upheavals. Yet it seems to me that Ghana is better understood by a different division of periods: Ghana was ahead of the rest, and its experience of the anticolonial struggle was generally a richer one. The years between Nkrumah's return in 1947 and the "turning points" in Ghana affairs that fell in 1960–61 can be seen in retrospect to make a single period of trend and action. The years after 1960 make another.

Within this "second period," onwards from 1960, the end of the Nkrumah regime was to be signaled by a strangely sordid and provincial drama. Running a little ahead of my story, I introduce it here as a useful though unpleasant note of punctuation.

Toward three o'clock on the morning of February 24, 1966, a small column of motorized infantry under the command of a soldier well enough known to be a vigorous opponent of the Nkrumah regime, Colonel Kotoka, came to a silent halt on the outskirts of Accra, having traveled through the night from its garrison headquarters at Kumase. The colonel got down and harangued his troops. There are varying accounts of what he said to them. But it seems that he told them they must now overthrow the regime because Nkrumah would otherwise send them to fight against the Americans in Vietnam. Possibly Kotoka believed this fairy tale; more probably, he did not. To that end, he went on, they must storm the President's offices at Flagstaff House, a complex of administrative buildings surrounded by a wall and guarded by other units of the Ghana armed forces, including men of a special security detachment. They must do this at once, furthermore, because Nkrumah had just left Ghana for the Far East.

Exhortation was one thing; action another. The colonel's column had neither mortars nor armored fighting vehicles: without these it would be difficult and perhaps impossible to carry Flagstaff House against a garrison that would fight. Contact was made with the army commanders in Accra. At first, it appears, these withheld their assent and were seized by the rebels; one of these commanders was incontinently shot down and killed.

As the night wore on, this situation changed.

General Ankrah, a former chief of staff whom Nkrumah had placed in retirement and who was acting in collusion with Kotoka, succeeded in persuading active commanders to back the *coup*. At the same time the chief of police also threw in his lot with the rebels.

Flagstaff House was attacked while dawn was breaking. Its defenders held firm. Among the wilder rumors afterwards put in circulation was one saying that these defenders included Russian officers. The loyal troops were all Ghanaian. They fought off the rebels through that day. But they were overcome, and by nightfall the *coup* was virtually complete. All that remained was to round up the regime's more prominent supporters and pack them into the prison cells from which the Nkrumah regime's political prisoners were now released.

Draconic penalties were announced against all or anyone who might speak a word in favor of Nkrumah, or might possess or be suspected of possessing any contact, however indirect, with anyone who might speak such a word.

The country as a whole accepted the *coup* with a silence that bespoke a profound indifference: the same kind of indifference that would afterwards accompany the next military *coup*, that of 1972, when the subsequent parliamentary regime was to be overthrown. The people as a whole—can one speak of a people as a whole? at least, by all the evidence, a large majority—watched the drama but evidently felt it no concern of theirs. The only great rejoicing, and this was brief, occurred in well-known centers of opposition to the CPP, among tribalists of Accra and traditionalists of Kumase.

This apparent indifference—one may even say this real indifference—is, I think, the core of what one has to consider and explain. It is very much a central part of the Ghana that Strand has photographed, or of the wider African scene for which his portrait validly stands. The people, or at any rate a large proportion of the people, had become indifferent, angry or disgusted. Moreover, they would largely remain thus, long after Nkrumah had ceased to govern. Yet they had not felt like this a dozen or so years earlier. What had produced the change? Important "turning points," as I have suggested, may be located in 1961.

One of these, certainly the most dramatic, was the unofficial strike by port workers at Takoradi—then the only deep-water port on the Ghana seaboard, and therefore vital to the country's economy. The strike held firm for much longer than was generally thought possible, but was defeated in the end; several of its leaders were arrested under preventive detention regulations.

But although this obscure stoppage was soon over, it made its mark. For it sharply spotlighted the wide gap that now existed and was felt to exist between the regime and its beneficiaries on one side, and the people on the other: in this case, that section of the people which formed the only real nucleus of an industrial working class in the Ghana of the early 1960's. The leading strikers were among those who had given victory to the CPP ten years earlier. Now they were contemptuously labeled as "rats" by Nkrumah's newly appointed aide, Tawia Adamafio, and it appeared that the regime as a whole was of this opinion.

Real wages had scarcely risen since the outright colonial period; in some cases they had fallen. The incomes of the majority of cocoa farmers had fared no better. Yet the traders and other beneficiaries who had taken over the CPP, increasingly after about 1952 or 1953, were in a quite different case. They had prospered. They had also seen to it, responding to their own social traditions, that everyone should know that they had prospered. Ministers who had been penniless a dozen years earlier were now the owners of mansions filled with expensive furniture as well as strangely ostentatious knickknacks whose cost was probably as great as their vulgarity. Money had become king; and money now made the rules, even if this meant bending everyone who could be bent.

A little later, in 1962, the opposition spokesman, Dr. Kofi Busia, would volunteer as a witness before an "anti-subversion committee" of the United States 87th Congress. Senator Dodd would say to him: "I take it that it is your opinion that Ghana is the center for subversive Communist activities in Western Africa, is that right?" And Dr. Busia, going to the support of those who wished to persuade Congress not to give aid to Ghana, would reply: "Mr. Chairman, I have stated this many times. . . ."

Leaving aside the possibly interesting question of Dr. Busia's motives in thus testifying against his own country, the exchange showed a curious if perhaps characteristic blindness. Nkrumah, it is true, had lately led the way in independent Africa by entering upon aid-and-trade relations with the U.S.S.R. and with other countries in the Soviet bloc. Perhaps it was this that had induced Senator Dodd to lead off, when hearing Busia, with a statement that Ghana had become "the mortal enemy of true freedom and independence for the peoples of Africa and the mortal enemy of African peace." And perhaps it was the same policies that induced Busia to agree with Dodd in words that left no possible doubt of Busia's agreement. Yet what Ghana had really become, by then, was the scene of subversive commercial rather than political activities among many, Ghanaian or not, who were able to embark on them; and their numbers, as it happened, were not few.

Nkrumah had marked this, if Busia had not, and earlier, in April 1961, had moved against it verbally. He then spoke angrily over the radio against CPP members who made it a habit "to go around the country in a bid to get rich quick by threatening people and collecting money from them . . . a most vicious and shameful practice"; but a practice that went together, by this time, with widespread commercial corruption and other forms of "primitive accumulation" of private wealth. Going on from there, Nkrumah introduced a rule whereby a CPP member should own no more than two houses totaling £20,000 in value, or more than two cars, or any plots of land worth more than £500. As a means of impressing wage earners living on or below the poverty line—and that is where most wage earners were living—this could only seem a sorry mocking of their plight.

Worse followed. The government brought in an "austerity budget" designed to provide additional public revenue. All wage earners were to lose 5 percent of their wages, deducted at source. Other types of "accessible income" were to lose 10 percent, similarly deducted wherever possible. This was aimed largely at cocoa farmers, some of whom were comparatively rich but most of whom were not, and all of whom, in any case, were already toughly taxed by the price mechanism of state cocoa-purchasing. The austerity budget was what provoked the Takoradi strike. Over and beyond doing that, however, it was a budget which dramatized the alienation of the regime from everyday realities. It marked the opening of a period in which the mass of ordinary people evidently felt themselves derided and oppressed.

Nkrumah's government, and other governments later, were to be well aware of this and were to try to deal with it in various ways. Independence had brought many good things, but it had also brought a deepening contrast in living standards between the rulers and the ruled, or, as political scientists were soon to phrase it, between "elites and masses." The reasons why it had done this must be sought in the detailed policies of those years, and this is not the place to discuss them. One may note, however, that the case was a general one. There was not a single newly independent country where this painfully widening gap failed to appear; and this was so because all of them had followed the prescriptions of advisers who believed that economic "take-off" into sustained growth could become possible only by obedience to the rules of "free enterprise." But instead of "take-off" there was crash in country after country, as disgusted or enraged people, or simply other people on the make, turned in anger against regime after regime.

Nkrumah, for his part, had the vision to foresee that crash could be avoided, and "take-off" become possible, only by following quite different rules. This led him into the bad books of such persons as Senator Dodd and Dr. Busia, as of everyone else prepared to believe their fantasies. But Nkrumah did not lack for courage. He persisted after 1961 with policies intended to change the rules. He spoke much of socialism in a country without any socialists. He set forth to train socialists. He wrote books explaining why the policies of the 1950's were no more than "neo-colonialist" prescriptions for maintaining an old foreign supremacy in a new guise.

In all this he failed. His analysis may have been sound, but his socialist policies turned out to be the feeble prophylaxis of an inefficient state capitalism. His newly trained socialists, with some honorable exceptions, proved nothing of the kind. He himself

became increasingly isolated from the facts of everyday life. He worked harder than ever, but now he worked quite often in a political vacuum. He remained true to his vision of a united Africa moving toward socialism, but the vision retreated like a mirage.

He and his work continued to possess the qualities of an impressive sincerity in these years after 1961, yet nothing that he did or tried to do was able to reverse the tide of troubles. Much that he did, or allowed others to do, only multiplied those troubles. The state became more oppressive; it also became more corrupt. In January 1964 he presided over a national referendum which was to confirm his presidency and make Ghana a one-party state. The voting figures officially returned gave 2,773,920 affirmative votes and 2,452 negative votes. Nobody believed the honesty of these returns; and, of course, they were not honest. But they were officially accepted, and the CPP became Ghana's only political party. Given what had now become the more or less total degeneration of the CPP as a democratic party, Ghana did not become a one-party state. Ghana became a no-party state. The results were predictable; they were also sad.

Finally, in 1965, the world price of cocoa nosedived, and the country was in economic crisis. By the end of that year, there were many who took it more or less for granted that Nkrumah's overthrow could now be only a question of time. Very few were surprised when it came the following month.

Those who had blamed Nkrumah and his post-1960 policies for the crisis and its accompanying troubles now had a chance to show what they themselves could do. There followed about three years of a military rule which did little more than temporize. General Ankrah and his men were active in prosecuting all those whom they could seize for corruption, but they were dealing with a system in which certain forms of corruption had become endemic; and one or two of these commanders duly fell victim to the very evils they were supposed to be rooting out. Otherwise, they merely reversed Nkrumah's policies of socialism, or rather of state capitalism, and eventually handed over power to a parliamentary regime.

This reversion to the "European model" appeared to begin well, in 1969, with elections generally thought to be honest and representative. But it was soon noticed that in reverting to the "European model" the new rulers had also called back those destructive tendencies towards "tribalism" and regionalism that Nkrumah and the early CPP governments had worked so hard, and on the whole so well, to eradicate or reduce. No economic genius, Dr. Busia as prime minister embarked on policies of foreign borrowing which soon outdid Nkrumah's much-condemned "excesses" in that direction. The economic situation worsened with every "orthodox policy" pursued by Dr. Busia's government.

Some fearful things were done. Among these was the expulsion of upwards of a million Nigerians, most of them long resident in Ghana, who were now said to be taking jobs and incomes from Ghanaian nationals, an act of xenophobic opportunism that Nkrumah would never have countenanced. Ghana became a small provincial country turned in upon itself and stranded on the verge of African affairs, instead of the small heroic country which had led the way to independence. Nothing showed this more painfully, it was said, than the cap-in-hand attitudes of the parliamentary regime toward its foreign patrons.

Whatever else he had done or not done, Nkrumah had given his people a profound pride and sense of confidence in their ability to stand level with the world, and go the way that seemed best to them. If this essay has had so much to say about Nkrumah, it is because the story of his country has been inseparable from his own story at a thousand vital points. His strengths were their strengths; his faults were their faults; his achievements and his failures were also very much their own. They had enjoyed his eminence in the world—and above all in that world where the assertion of African equality was such a new thing—because it was also their own eminence.

Perhaps Busia would have been forgiven for much that he did if only his capitalism had worked. But it did nothing of the kind. He borrowed long and he borrowed short. He went to extraordinary lengths to reassure his creditors. Yet nothing availed. Busia found that he had to devalue the Ghana currency. This he did overnight, by 48 percent. The soldiers moved

against him almost at once.

These new soldiers were a different sort of men from those who had ousted Nkrumah. They were younger and therefore less tied to colonial traditions and loyalties. They had the advantage of having watched the successive efforts of the Ankrah regime of 1966 and after, and then the Busia regime, in trying to overcome crisis by restoring the "European model." They had seen this culminate in a disastrous devaluation which they now hastened to cancel in favor of a much smaller one. They had also watched Busia denouncing the "Nkrumah debts" while piling up his own. They began to embark on experiments of their own; and with these they have persevered.

Ghana is no longer a country in crisis. The problems that Nkrumah began to face in 1960 have still to be resolved. But now, at least, these problems are again seen as Nkrumah saw them: problems which have their roots in deep and difficult questions of historical and modern structure. In this, these soldiers seem well aware that Ghana is not alone. Their government has begun to develop a willingness to stand back and consider problems in a long perspective.

Just how the people of Ghana now think about all this may still be something they prefer to keep to themselves. If it is, then their "silence" may be attributable to nothing more sinister than a preference for reassuring visitors that all is well, and for keeping one's troubles in the family. What appears to be true, in any case, is that all the upheavals and experiences and joys and sorrows of the past twenty years of independence from foreign rule have now indeed reduced the period of that rule to the dimensions of an episode. They have reduced it to an episode in the background of a national consciousness which sees its present and unfolding problems in the light of its own history, loyalties and choices: a consciousness which begins to inspire, once again, the search for appropriate solutions.

NINE SO SHALL WE SAY...?

Waiting in Wa for the words to appear, while supping at the pleasure of THE NEW EPICURE and the cook's cunning mastery of that venerable appliance, I had not thought it likely that they would include all these facts and facts. Afterwards, it was tempting to close away the books and merely talk about the scene. That would have limped along behind Strand's camera. But I have to admit that the temptation was a strong one.

Many have felt this temptation, and in a variety of moods. Europeans have felt it, Asians have felt it, white Americans have felt it; so have black Americans, frequent visitors to Ghana now and sometimes visitors who come to stay. Many of all these people have responded with admiration, some with disappointment, a few with words that reach across the years. It would have pleased my old acquaintance, the famous chief of the Akan who could not stand Nkrumah, that among the last of these categories was a granddaughter of Queen Victoria: a princess of the blood, no less. "It is a marvellous country," reported Princess Marie Louise in 1925. "What is its spell? I cannot tell you, nor wherein lies its . . . unfathomable charm. It lays its hand upon you, and, having felt its compelling strength, you never can forget it or be wholly free of it. . . ."

So shall we say that this is what Ghana is really like, that this is what Africa is really like? Did the princess see the pit latrines and smell the open sewers, and, if so, merely dismiss them as a stage upon humanity's journey to the toilets of Windsor? Did she glimpse the grasping fist of extended-family despotism, and, if so, merely recall that royal families can be like that, too? Did she inspect the poverty and deprivation, and think them picturesque? I really cannot tell you, for I have no idea what kind of person she was, that princess. But I enjoy her words even if they are romantic, or just because they are romantic. They are the kind of words that can make a bridge between reality and its perception. There is nothing in the least romantic about Ghana—or, come to that, about any other part of Africa—for those who have experienced its hard

and highly realistic hand. All the same, those who see only the clenched knuckles and the anxious palm may need a little help with their perceptions, and the romantic vision can be a useful one from time to time.

Or shall we say that all this is vastly overdone, and Africa greatly overwritten, and Ghana an optical illusion of the "village butterflies"? This may be rather in the fashion nowadays, especially among those who saw the romantic vision but not the knuckles and the palm. That seems a pity, although Africa will scarcely care. If Africans are aware of this mood, they may even enjoy its irony, for irony is among their strong suits of characteristic response. Having seen "nothing" in Africa for so long, the disillusioned then saw "everything" but did not find it, and now are sad or sorry. To continue a little with Efua's story:

There was a woman long ago,
Tell that maid, tell that maid,
There was a woman long ago,
She would not marry Kwesi
She would not marry Kwaw,
She would not, would not, would not . . .

Tell that maid, tell that maid,
Her man looked like a chief
Most splendid to see
But he turned into a python
He turned into a python
And swallowed her up.

So shall we say, shall we put it that way? The photographs in this book should have the last word, and they make no such answer. If there is a "mystery" about Africa, and I rather think that when everything has been said and done there is, then they reveal this mystery; and what they reveal, or so it seems to me, is neither a charm that is "strange and unfathomable," nor a "spell" that "lays its hand upon you," much less an optical illusion, but features and reflections of humanity which are not common to us all, not in the least common to us all, yet in which all of us can recognize ourselves. Among many virtues, Strand's work never "mystifies," never "overwrites," never misleads, but shows and suggests and continually enhances that patient contemplation of appearance which discovers truth. What he gives us is the tone and fabric of that appearance, but, penetrating beyond that, the reality of its strength as well. Here we can share an insight which contains the mastery that will endure.

Of the following short introductory list of recent or relatively recent books about Ghana, several have extensive bibliographies:

Older History

A. Adu Boahen, *Topics in West African History*, Longman, London, 1966.

J. F. Ade Ajayi and M. Crowder (eds.), *History of West Africa*, 2 vols., Longman, London, 1971, 1974.

P. D. Curtin, *The Atlantic Slave Trade: A Census*, Wisconsin University Press, Madison, 1969.

J. D. Fage, *Ghana: A Historical Interpretation*, Wisconsin University Press, Madison, 1959.

K. Yeboa Daaku, *Trade and Politics on the Gold Coast, 1600–1720*, Clarendon, Oxford, 1970.

B. Davidson, *A History of West Africa to the 19th Century*, Longman, London, and Doubleday, New York, 1966.

———, *Black Mother: The African Slave Trade*, Atlantic-Little, Brown, Boston, and Gollancz, London, 1961.

D. Kimble, *A Political History of Ghana, 1850–1928*, Clarendon, Oxford, 1963.

A. W. Lawrence, *Trade Castles and Forts of West Africa*, Cape, London, 1963.

M. Priestley, *West African Trade and Coast Society*, Oxford University Press, 1969.

E. Reynolds, *Trade and Economic Change on the Gold Coast, 1807–1874*, Longman, London, 1974.

W. E. F. Ward, *A History of Ghana*, Allen & Unwin, London, 1958.

I. Wilks, *Asante in the Nineteenth Century*, Cambridge University Press, 1975.

Newer History

A. A. Afrifa, *The Ghana Coup: 24 February 1966*, with introductions by K. A. Busia and T. Szamuely, Cass, London, 1966.

D. E. Apter, *The Gold Coast in Transition*, Princeton, 1955.

D. Austin, *Politics in Ghana, 1946–60*, Oxford University Press, 1970.

G. Bing, *Reap the Whirlwind (Ghana: 1950–66)*, MacGibbon & Kee, London, 1968.

W. Birmingham, I. Neustadt, E. N. Omaboe, *A Study of Contemporary Ghana: Vol. 1, The Economy of Ghana; Vol. 2, Some Aspects of Social Structure*, Allen & Unwin, London, 1966, 1967.

F. M. Bourret, *The Gold Coast*, Oxford University Press, 1949.

B. Davidson, *Black Star: A View of the Life and Times of Kwame Nkrumah*, Longman, London, and Praeger, New York, 1973.

B. Fitch and M. Oppenheimer, *Ghana: End of an Illusion*, Monthly Review Press, New York, 1966.

P. Hill, *The Gold Coast Cocoa Farmer*, Oxford University Press, 1956.

———, *Studies in Rural Capitalism in West Africa*, Cambridge University Press, 1970.

T. Hodgkin, *Nationalism in Colonial Africa*, Muller, London, 1956.

R. Makonnen, *Pan-Africanism from Within*, as recorded and edited by K. King, Oxford University Press, 1973.

R. Szerezewski, *Structural Changes in the Economy of Ghana, 1851–1911*, Weidenfeld & Nicolson, London, 1965.

W. S. Thompson, *Ghana's Foreign Policy, 1957–66*, Princeton University Press, 1969.

M. Wight, *The Gold Coast Legislative Council*, Faber, London, 1947.

R. Wright, *Black Power*, Dobson, London, 1956.

Nationalist Writings

A comprehensive list would be a long one. Those wanting a wide-ranging and reliable guide should consult: J. Ayodele Langley, *Pan-Africanism and Nationalism in West Africa, 1900–45*, Clarendon, Oxford, 1973. Meanwhile, here are a few early and late titles:

S. R. B. Attoh Ahuma, *The Gold Coast Nation and National Consciousness*, with introduction by J. C. de Graft-Johnson, 1911; reprinted by Cass, London, 1971.

J. E. Casely Hayford, *Ethiopia Unbound, 1911*, with introduction by F. B. Ugonna; reprinted by Cass, London, 1971.

J. Africanus Horton, *West African Countries and Peoples, 1868*, with introduction by G. Shepperson; reprinted by Edinburgh University Press, 1969.

K. Nkrumah, *Autobiography*, Nelson, London, 1957.

———, *Africa Must Unite*, Heinemann, London, 1963.

———, *Consciencism*, Heinemann, London, 1964.

The Arts

Prose and poetry flourish in Ghana as in other African countries. Readers who want an introduction might consult:

Voices of Ghana: Literary Contributions to the Ghana Broadcasting System, 1955–57, Government Printer, Accra, 1958.

O. R. Dathorne and W. Feuser (eds.), *Africa in Prose*, Penguin Books, London and Baltimore, 1969.

G. Moore and U. Beier (eds.), *Modern Poetry from Africa*, Penguin Books, London and Baltimore, 1963.

Frank Kobina Parkes, *Songs from the Wilderness*, University of London Press, 1965.

In the context of this book one may single out a vivid novel by:

A. Kwei Armah, *The Beautyful Ones Are Not Yet Born*, Heinemann, London, 1968.

On the plastic arts there is much to be learned from:

W. Fagg and E. Elisofon, *The Sculpture of Africa*, Thames & Hudson, London, 1958.

A. A. Y. Kyerematen, *Panoply of Ghana*, Longman, London, 1964.

J. H. K. Nketia, *The Music of Africa*, Gollancz, London, 1975.

M. W. Plass, *The Goldweights of the Ashanti*, Lund Humphries, London, 1967.

A distinguished discussion and illustration of another art is:

L. Prussin, *Architecture in Northern Ghana*, University of California Press, 1969.

Religions, Shrine-healing, Structures, etc.

K. A. Busia, *Report on a Social Survey of Sekondi-Takoradi*, Government Printer, Accra, 1950.

B. Davidson, *The African Genius: An Introduction to Social and Cultural History* Atlantic - Little, Brown, Boston, 1969; as *The Africans*, Longman, London, 1969.

M. Field, *Religion and Medicine of the Ga People*, Oxford University Press, 1937.

———, *Search for Security: An Ethno-psychiatric Study of Rural Ghana*, Faber, London, 1960.

M. Fortes, *The Dynamics of Clanship Among the Tallensi*, Oxford University Press, 1945.

———, *The Web of Kinship Among the Tallensi*, Oxford University Press, 1949.

J. Goody, *Technology, Tradition and the State in Africa*, Oxford University Press, 1971.

R. S. Rattray, *Ashanti Proverbs*, Oxford University Press, 1916.

———, *Ashanti*, Oxford University Press, 1923.

———, *Religion and Art in Ashanti*, Oxford University Press, 1927.

D. Tait, *The Konkomba of Northern Ghana*, Oxford University Press, 1961.

Aperture thanks those publishers and individuals who have kindly given their permission to use the following texts to which they hold the copyright:

David E. Apter, "Admonitions to Ghanaian Chiefs," from *Ghana in Transition*, second revised edition, Princeton University Press, 1972, pp. 112–113.

Kofii Awoonor, "Song of War," from *Modern Poetry from Africa*, Penguin Books, London and Baltimore, 1963.

J. A. Braimah and J. R. Goody, "Nazm al-la'ali bi-akhbar wa tanbih al-kiram," from *Salaga: The Struggle for Power*, Longman, London, 1967.

Kwesi Brew, "The Search," from *Modern Poetry from Africa*, Penguin Books, London and Baltimore, 1963.

J. Ayodele Langley, "Gold Coast Soldier's Parody of Psalm 23," from *Pan-Africanism and Nationalism in West Africa, 1900–1945*, Clarendon Press, London, 1972. "Psalm 23" first appeared in *African Morning Post* (Accra, 2 September 1944); reprinted in *WASU Magazine* (1944).

Albert Kayper Mensah, "A Second Birthday," from *Voices of Ghana*, Government Printer, Accra, 1958, p. 57.

Kwame Nkrumah, *Africa Must Unite*, Panaf Books, London, 1963, p. 193.

———, *Autobiography of Kwame Nkrumah*, Panaf Books, London, 1957; all rights reserved.

E. E. Obeng, "Konaduwa's Trial," from *Eighteenpence*, Arthur Stockwell, Ilfracombe, 1943, pp. 37–44.

Andrew Amankwa Opoku, "Afram," from *Voices of Ghana*, Government Printer, Accra, 1958, p. 77.

Frank Kobina Parkes, "African Heaven," from *Songs from the Wilderness*, University of London Press, 1965.

R. S. Rattray, "A story from Asante" and "Asante maxim," from *Ashanti Proverbs*, Oxford University Press, 1916.

Efua Theodora Sutherland, "New Life at Kyerefaso," from *Voices of Ghana*, Government Printer, Accra, 1958, p. 204.

I. Wilks, "The Asantehene Osei Bonsu," from *Asante in the Nineteenth Century*, Cambridge University Press, 1975, p. 685.

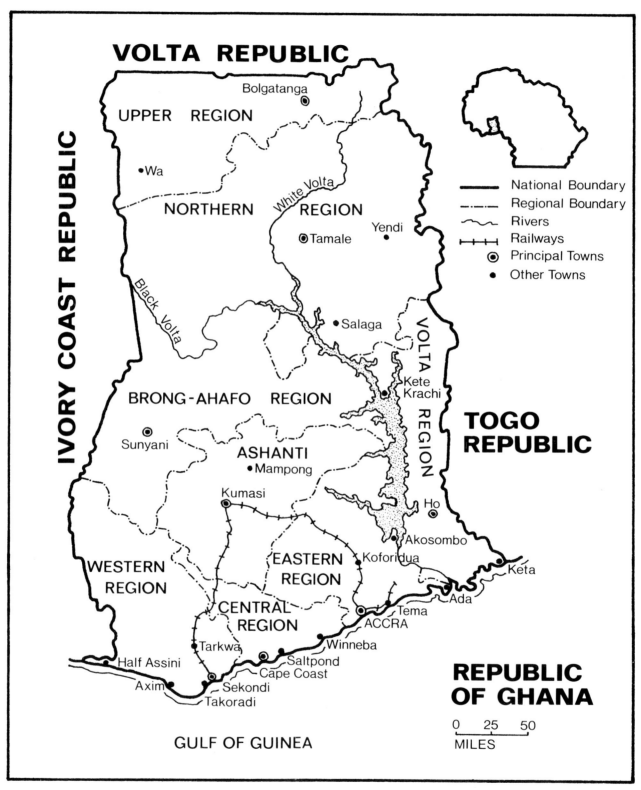

VOLTA REPUBLIC

IVORY COAST REPUBLIC

UPPER REGION

Bolgatanga

•Wa

NORTHERN

White Volta

REGION

⊙Tamale

Yendi

Black Volta

•Salaga

National Boundary
Regional Boundary
Rivers
Railways
⊙ Principal Towns
• Other Towns

VOLTA REGION

BRONG-AHAFO REGION

Kete
Krachi

TOGO
REPUBLIC

⊙
Sunyani

ASHANTI

•Mampong

Ho

Kumasi

Akosombo

WESTERN
REGION

EASTERN
REGION

Koforidua

Keta

CENTRAL
REGION

Ada

Tema
ACCRA

Tarkwa

Winneba

REPUBLIC
OF GHANA

Half Assini

Saltpond
Cape Coast

Axim

Sekondi
Takoradi

0   25   50
MILES

GULF OF GUINEA